BEHIND ENEMY LINES
Mickey Edwards

**A rebel in Congress
proposes a bold new politics
for the 1980s**

Regnery Gateway
Chicago

Published by Regnery Gateway, Inc.,
360 West Superior Street
Chicago, Illinois 60610-0890

Edwards, Mickey, 1937-
  Behind Enemy Lines

  1. United States. Congress. 2. United States—Politics and government—1981- I. Title.
JK1061.E38 1983 328.73 82-42904 ISBN 0-89526-621-0

BEHIND ENEMY LINES

A rebel in Congress proposes a bold new politics for the 1980s

AN OLDE VERSE

The law doth punish man or woman
That steals the goose from the common,
But lets the greater felon loose
That steals the common from the goose.

A PERSONAL NOTE

To Lisa, who has brought me so much.

I met Lisa Reagan in mid-air and we've been there ever since. We were somewhere between Oklahoma City and St. Louis on a TWA flight bound, eventually, for Washington. It was January the 18th, 1981, two days before the inauguration of a new President.

Lisa cared, and cares, about politics as much as I care about the fig-growing season in southern Lebanon. This new President was, in some distant way—third cousin or fourth—a relative of hers, the first in the Reagan family to achieve such widespread notoriety, and that fact, rather than some passion for born-again pre-Keynesian economics, had been her principal reason for working her way into a group of Oklahomans heading east for the inauguration. Lisa is a singer, a good one, a former Miss Oklahoma who had won a talent award in the Miss America pageant. Her life's interests were centered around music, not politics, and if she didn't know macroeconomics from macaroni we were even because I wouldn't have known a diva from a divot.

The previous year had been the hardest of my life. Sometime during a hazy, blurred winter of 1979, fuzzy, indistinct months in which too much pain and too many tears became melted together, my wife, Sue, had told me she wanted a divorce.

Sue had worked hard to help elect me to the Congress, and she loved and enjoyed politics. But after three years with hardly a weekend or an evening together, Sue wanted something different for her life. What she wanted was normalcy. A single home in a single city. A husband who was home at 5:00. A husband to spend the evenings and the weekends and the holidays with her. I've tried very hard to blame her for feeling that way, but I can't.

Our marriage had once been a good one, and the experiences we shared together fill this book. I tried very hard to save that marriage. I offered to resign from the Congress and never run again, a decision I would make today rather than let my family slip imperceptibly, inadvertently, into second place in my life. But it was too late; we had seen each other too seldom, lived through too many experiences, from campaign speeches to school plays, without each other. The love she had once had for me had been buried fractions of an inch at a time under the blizzard of a Congressional schedule, speeches, meetings, trips, obligatory appearances at parades, dedications, and civic club luncheons.

I learned that Sue's decision was final by telephone. She was at home, on a weekend, in the winter, in Washington. I was in a small hotel room in New Hampshire, cold, exhausted after a weekend of campaigning for Ronald Reagan. The miles and the cold made for great symbolism that night; Steinbeck could not have amplified on that winter of our discontent.

I do not blame Sue; she was sincere in what she wanted for her life and soon after we were divorced she married an Air Force sergeant and moved to southern California. Instead, I blamed my job, politics, government, my constituents, the philosophies I had felt so passionate about, the conservative political movement to which I had given so much time and to which I had ultimately sacrificed far more than I meant to.

I returned to Washington after the elections of 1980 with a sense of distance from the battles I had fought, the flags I had carried, the causes I had helped to lead. My compassions were smothered by a sense of feeling sorry for myself that outweighed my sorrow for others. My charges up the hills of conflict were slowed by uncertainty that the victory—or defeat—really counted for very much among the truly important things of life.

I retreated to a corner, personally and politically, and nursed my wounds.

On January 20th Ronald Reagan became President and Lisa Reagan came to my office, which had become a gathering spot for Oklahomans who were in town for the inauguration. I'm not much for parades or parties and certainly had no intention of attending the inaugural parade, which promised to be interminable. That was the first of many such decisions which have since been modified.

Our first "date" consisted of walking some 25 or 30 blocks to the parade stands which had been set up near the White House. Lisa was in high heels. I had absolutely no idea how to get over, through or around the barricades and barriers that had been set up along the way. We arrived less than a minute before the parade did. It was not the kind of first date one might plan. I did buy her a gift, though—an awful-looking souvenir cap consisting of an upraised elephant's trunk extending from the area that usually says "International Harvester" or "Billy Bob's Feed and Seed" and two floppy "elephant ears" hanging down from the sides. I suppose Lisa decided I was too strange to be allowed to wander the streets without protection. We got married a few months later.

Lisa has a strong Christian faith and a deep reservoir of character that I was able to grab and hold onto like a lifeline thrown from a passing ship. Our faith, our love, our home, and now somebody new in our lives, Patrick Daniel, an "egg with legs", our fat little red-headed Polish-Irish son, these things have become a new focal point in my life. Tuesday night Bible studies and Monday-through-Sunday tunafish and leftovers at home have replaced meetings, parties, and receptions. I dedicate this book to Lisa because she has rekindled fires that had gone out. In a world of silk and plastic, Lisa is cotton and oak. She still prefers metronomes to macroeconomics, but that's alright; I have always preferred E. B. White, Shostakovich and Edna St. Vincent Millay to Laffer curves myself.

Ironically, though, placing the first priority where it belongs has made me better able to do my job in the Congress, happily, eagerly, and well, than I was ever able to do before.

To Lisa, then.

And to the glory of God, who forgives us so much and who gives us each so many more chances than we deserve.

On March 24, 1983, just two months before this book was due to be released, and before she could read it, my mother died in a California hospital. For six months she had fought for life from a hospital bed—through cancer surgery, chemotherapy, a heart attack, kidney failure, blood infections and pneumonia. My mother was 70, small, quiet, and, in many ways, timid. To the day she died—24 years after she moved to the Los Angeles suburbs—she refused to drive on the city's frightening freeways. She moved slowly and she seldom exerted herself needlessly. But, oh, what an inner strength she had. And what a beauty. She simply never complained. When her children were thoughtless; when they did strange and inexplicable things—when I was divorced; when I became a Christian—the only Christian, probably, in the history of our wonderfully, joyously Jewish family; even when I became a politician (our family had always been poor; "who are we," she once asked, "to have a Congressman in the family?"), through all this she simply smiled, shrugged, and loved. In her last days, when the pain was more intense, the nurses and doctors knew that if Rosie bothered them to ask for a pill or a shot the pain must be bad, indeed. From all over the ward they gathered at her bed when she died, and they cried. What a symbol of quiet suffering and inner strength my amazing mother had become. My mother had been a widow for nearly a quarter of a century and never even went out with another man. She was Eddie Edwards' girl and wanted only to be with him again. Now she is. Rosalie Videtsky Miller Edwards—my sweet Momma—this book is for you, too.

Part One
BEHIND ENEMY LINES

CHAPTER ONE:
LIBERAL DREAMS, CONSERVATIVE CAUTION: CREATING A POLITICAL FUSION

1. The Failure of Liberalism, The Silence of Conservatism

For as long as I can remember, I've had a disturbing perspective of government not as a friendly uncle but as a neighborhood bully, lying in wait to snatch away the lunch money, or as the community busybody (I always picture somebody who looks like Margaret Hamilton, the wicked witch in the Wizard of Oz) .

And then I was elected to Congress.

For years I had seen government as the enemy. Now I was suddenly behind the enemy lines. *Inside* the enemy camp, in fact.

I sit in Congress incongruous, a Conservative in a Congress which is not. Much of what the Congress does is done because my body does not stop many of the enemy tanks it is thrown before. I merely get a lot of tracks across my back.

Sometimes, though, when that tank rolls over us, something happens and the legislative machine is momentarily derailed. In the Congress, each tank that doesn't reach its target is a victory for the people.

And so I find myself a private in the ranks of the enemy, fighting my own war from within.

Getting ready for work in the morning, preparing to face the enemy, I pick music to psych myself, to stir the blood and send the adrenalin pumping through my veins. Aaron Copland and Shostakovich, "Rocky" and "Star Wars." I think of Mo Udall and Tip O'Neill while Luke Skywalker charges toward the Starship, while Rocky prepares for the fight. I listen to Scherhezade and charge, with Sinbad, toward Washington.

(Having acquired some experience in the business of psychologically preparing myself for doing battle with the Enemy, I offer this list of readily available works that will get the job done: Glazunov, *Symphony No. 5*; Hindemith, *Mathis der Mahler*; Janacek, *Taras Bulba*; Prokofiev, *Symphony No. 5*; Saint-Saens, *Symphony No. 3*; Schumann, *Symphony No. 1*; Shostakovich, *Symphony No. 11*; Strauss; *Ein Heldenleben*, and, of course, *Rocky, Star Wars*, and almost anything by Rachmaninoff, Offenbach or Tchaikovsky.)

I hope, of course, that this book will be well-received, but I am reminded of one critic's review of the great Gogol's first book, *Hans Kuechelgarten*: "The publisher of this book says that it was not intended for publication but that imperative considerations led the author to change his mind...considerations still more imperative should have restrained him."

One can merely do his best and take his chances.

This is a book about the United States Congress. No other institution anywhere in the world affects you quite as much, whether you're black or white; rich or poor; cabbie or cowboy. In it, 535 men and women decide directly or indirectly, in one way or another, how much you pay in taxes, whether and when and where we will go to war, whether you—or your children—will be drafted to fight in a war if we have one, and, to a large extent, how much you pay for bread, cheese, milk, meat, Chryslers, Toyotas, bicycles, lawnmowers and the two-story, split-level, ranch-style or colonial home in the suburbs that became a part of the American dream and then became too expensive for most Americans to buy.

The United States Congress has created the mess we're in. It is one of the least respected, least trusted institutions in America. Yet the people in it are re-elected with amazing consistency.

I sometimes think geography teachers ought to include Washington in their class outlines as a foreign city. It's often as remote as Pretoria or Rangoon.

The government—our government—too often is our enemy: the enemy of our dreams, our hopes, our aspirations. Things have changed somewhat in the years since I first came to Washington; the growth of government is slower today and even those people who created the massive spending programs now operating out of Washington are critical of the resulting national debt, which is a lot like a germ criticizing disease. But the federal government does continue to grow, and as it does, as the national debt exceeds a trillion dollars and America spends more than any other nation in the history of the world, America changes and its dreams fade.

The liberal experiment has failed; that is obvious. What comes next? What will be the politics of the 80s? After 50 years of liberal politics, blacks remain outside the system, women only on the fringes of it, and blue-collar America has had its dreams snatched away. It is time for new ideas, new approaches.

But those ideas must have form, substance. Rhetoric cannot govern a nation. Private enterprise and individual initiative—the cornerstones of so-called "conservative" politics—can, indeed, help Americans achieve their aspirations: steady employment, growing savings accounts, retirement accounts, education, housing, health care. There is no question that the private sector can produce such miracles; that is its function.

But can it provide for at least the reasonable aspirations of *all* Americans? Can it provide for those who so frequently fall between the cracks as society rushes past? Those whose homes remain unheated in an energy-rich society? Those who cannot afford food in a land of abundant harvests?

After the 1980 elections a friend, Janet Blankenship, turned to me and said, with sympathy, wonder and warning: "You're like the dog that kept chasing the car. . . and finally caught it. Now that you've got it, you'd better know what to do with it."

The problem is, when one sits too long outside the decision-making process, reduced to the impotence of occasional shrugs and frequent complaints, one is likely to begin thinking of politics as "the science of complaining about what somebody else is doing."

In the 1970s, liberals came up with a scheme to do something about the high unemployment rate among black teenagers. It was called the Humphrey-Hawkins Bill. Conservatives later bragged that they had turned it into the 'umphrey-'awkins Bill "by knocking the H out of it" before it was passed.

I did not disagree with conservative opposition to the bill. Humphrey-Hawkins began by going too far—giving the federal government authority to set employment quotas—and was so often revised and diluted that it finally became meaningless, establishing a federal program to devise employment goals, but doing nothing whatsoever to bring them about. It seemed embarrassingly similar to the federally funded study to determine why children fall off bicycles (the study concluded, after months of research and thousands of tax dollars, that children fall off bicycles because they lose their balance).

But what was the *conservative* plan to do something about the high unemployment rate among black teenagers? Or, to put it in people terms, what did *we* propose to do about the fact that so many young people, trying to earn a living to help support their families, simply couldn't find anybody to hire them? Rhetoric and political philosophy aside, there was no conservative program to address that problem: most conservatives had never given serious thought to the fact that a lot of young black people were in desperate need of jobs. The conservative program consisted of opposition to the Humphrey-Hawkins Bill and a vague plea to "let the private sector take care of it."

That, in theory, is a proper response. It is, in fact, the very essence of conservative philosophy. Ultimately, taking steps to free the great potential of the private sector would create new businesses, new jobs, and new opportunities reaching deeply into every part of the society. The much-maligned "trickle-down" theory does work and is responsible for creating America's great industrial capability and a standard of living which by the middle of the twentieth century had become both the highest in the world and the most evenly distributed. When people invest and create businesses, and those businesses in turn create jobs and new, improved products, then people at lower economic levels receive both income and improved, lower-priced products. True, the money is not passed down the line evenly, and there will remain an enormous gulf between the income of the chairman of the board and the man on the assembly line, but as the benefits have trickled down, the man on the assembly line has moved up the financial ladder to a point unheard of in previous societies: factory workers, oilfield roughnecks, clerks are able to save for retirement, educate their children, take family vacations, own their own homes.

What's more, "trickle-down" is an accurate description only in terms of direction, not in terms of rate of flow. Benefits flow rather rapidly from investments in business and industry, and when the investments dry up, so do the benefits which flow to workers. During the Carter presidency, real business investment declined; the amount of money put into savings accounts, and thereby available for investment, declined to the lowest rate since the end of World War II; the gross national product declined. The result was predictable: unemployment soared. By the end of the Carter presidency, what had been a relatively low rate of unemployment only four years before had suddenly become a national tragedy: eight million Americans were out of work, and two years later, as a result of the declining business investment during the Carter years, unemployment was at more than 10 percent.

Something is always going to trickle down: either the positive results of investment or the negative results of the lack of investment.

Does that fact, however, justify conservatives responding to high rates of unemployment among minority teenagers with a simple appeal to let the private sector deal with the problem?

Private enterprise is the nub of a workable and desirable economic and political system, both the economic and political parts of which are based on the principle of laissez faire. But—and here is where conservatives fail—it is *only* a system, a skeleton upon which must be hung the flesh, blood and muscle of a society.

It is true that economic freedom will lead one to put maximum effort into those enterprises which will produce the greatest personal reward and that will create businesses which will create jobs which will create widespread well-being. And in theory employers will not mistreat their workers because that would cause them to look for work elsewhere. And there would always be someplace else for them to go, because other employers, seeking their own maximum profit, would realize quickly that a bit more generosity would allow them to steal away the competition's most skilled workers. Free enterprise does, indeed, work, and I place myself firmly in the ranks of its most ardent supporters.

But:

Let us imagine, difficult though it may be, a society in which there is a widespread disinclination to hire blacks. And let us further imagine that most blacks in that society, for one reason or another, are less well-educated and/or less skilled than non-blacks. In such a case will reliance on the private sector's pursuit of profit provide jobs for blacks? Will it give them a place to seek better employment if an employer proves not to be as generous as he should, in theory, be?

Let us imagine a widow, well along in years, past working age, with no money saved from her husband's modest salary or hers. Will reliance on the private sector's pursuit of profit provide for payment of her heating bills when winter comes?

The point is, private enterprise can, and does, provide a system, a framework, for widespread and heretofore unimaginable affluence. But there are holes in it, as there are with any system. Any society based on a spiritual foundation will have a high degree of charitable impulse which will prompt people to volunteer for church activities, contribute to the Boy Scouts and the local Arts League, and donate toys for the children of the needy at Christmas time. But, again, there will be holes in the foundation. All safety nets—all nets, by definition—have holes, no matter how small, and it is no betrayal of laissez faire economics nor of laissez faire politics to suggest that sometimes there is a need for positive steps by some social entity (preferably at the closest local level) to provide filler for those holes.

The problem has been that liberal solutions have permitted the government to intrude into society far beyond the involvement that would be required to fill the holes. As a result, government has both diminished freedom unnecessarily and, through overregulation, punched a few holes in the safety net where none existed before. Government has often lost sight of its original goal, which was to help people escape from poverty, and has begun instead simply to devise programs to help people exist more comfortably *in* poverty.

That failure of liberalism, however, does not excuse conservatives from dealing with the very real problems that exist in a society made up not of theories but of people. Unfortunately, some conservatives have spent so much time criticizing liberal solutions to those problems that they have lost sight of their own goals; they have forgotten to ask what kind of society *they* want to create in America.

We conservatives must begin to articulate more clearly and more frequently our own agenda for the future. If we are to continue to win elections and remain a political force in America, we must talk not merely of what we would change, but of what we would build. The American people will respond to a politics not of despair, but of hope.

Some conservatives have, in fact, been highly attentive to this need for a new socially-aware kind of conservatism. Congressman Jack Kemp, of New York, perhaps the best known of this group, rather than merely criticizing proposed liberal solutions to the problem of high rates of inner-city unemployment, borrowed an idea from the British and began to promote a system of Urban Enterprise Zones which would use the tax structure to encourage hiring in areas of high unemployment. It is not yet a perfect plan, and has run into some justifiable criticism, but it is at least a start based on sound conservative principles (less taxation and less regulation) *and* an awareness of an existing problem affecting a large part of the community.

Our goal must be to create a free society that is designed to help all people come as close as possible to achieving their maximum potential in life. The 1980s are going to require a revolutionary new kind of politics, a politics that simply ignores old labels and starts over.

"Conflicting" philosophies sometimes share similar goals, at least superficially. The liberal Paul Goodman, for example, once wrote: "I hold . . . that sovereign power must be diminished because it is too dangerous to live with; that people must be free of coercion in order to grow and adventure; that administration should be decentralized as much as possible." There are undoubtedly some conservatives who would disagree with that (some *prefer* an element of sovereign power in order to force people to do what conservatives would have them do), but most conservatives would embrace Goodman's sentence eagerly and (if no one found out where it came from) stick it into their own statements (as, in fact, I have just done).

There are areas in which political philosophies can be fused—or, at least, in which some of their differences can be bridged. The politics of the 1980s will require a philosophical blend that incorporates an instinctive liberal compassion; hard-nosed conservative insistence on fiscal sanity and on private, rather than public, enterprise; a libertarian passion for preserving freedom (both liberals and conservatives sometimes suggest preserving a free society by taking away freedoms), and a new kind of free enterprise populism which focuses not on big business but on small businesses and small farms, and which embraces free enterprise as a vehicle to create new economic opportunity for those who are still outside the system.

How does one create such a political fusion? M. Stanton Evans, one of the conservative movement's most articulate voices for the past 20 years, and somewhat of a fusionist himself, put it clearly: " . . . the pendulum does not swing of its own momentum; someone has to push it."

I'm trying to push the pendulum.

2. Shadows and Stress: How the Congress Really Works

The United States Congress is one of the most powerful institutions in the world and hardly anybody understands it at all—how it works, why if often doesn't work, who gets elected to Congress, how they get elected, or what motivates them after they get elected.

Everybody has a theory, of course.

Some—the suspicious types, obviously—believe that when members of Congress decide how to vote, they are responding to the whispered urgings of shifty-eyed men lurking in the shadows with pockets full of cash. Are there really such men, passing out locked briefcases or tightly-rolled Safeway sacks full of money?

One night late in 1962, a few miles outside a small Midwestern farm town, I watched as the vice president of a large eastern-based oil company pulled quietly into a dark clearing alongside a deserted country road and handed a campaign worker for a congressional candidate a cheap briefcase stuffed full of cash. Nearly twenty years later I watched a corporation president, in broad daylight, in mid-afternoon, in a modern downtown office building, hand a member of Congress a plain white unsealed Number 10 business envelope bulging with hundred-dollar bills.

But the exchange in the country took place before unreported paperbag contributions were illegal and, the Congressman, twenty years later, handed back the envelope without counting the cash or waiting to hear what strings, if any, might attend such a generous gift.

Do such things still happen? Almost certainly. There is ample evidence, ranging from Koreagate to Abscam, that larceny exists as surely in the hearts of some Congressmen as it does elsewhere in a society not greatly fettered by moral constraints.

In fact, there are shadows wherever one looks. William Natcher, of Kentucky, one of the most respected Members of the House, assumed the chairmanship of an Appropriations subcommittee after his legendary predecessor, Daniel Flood, had been indicted. Cappy Hollenbeck, of New Jersey, became a Congressman because his predecessor was indicted, convicted, and sent to prison. Frank Thompson, of New Jersey, was one of the most powerful men in the government when I arrived in Washington; he was defeated in 1980 after making his film debut on the FBI's Abscam tapes. Richard Kelley, of Florida, a former judge, was filmed stuffing wads of cash into his coat pockets; Edward Roybal, of California, was reprimanded for taking gifts from Tongsun Park. Ozzie Meyers, of Pennsylvania, became the first man to be expelled from the Congress in the 20th century, after he agreed to trade a little congressional influence for a little non-congressional cash.

No, if evil lurks in the hearts of men, then there is a fair share of it in the Congress as well.

Nor are members of Congress—even honest members of Congress—immune from other failings which leave them vulnerable to people who want to gain influence over them. The stress, the schedule, the travel, the frustration, the constant demands affect each member of Congress differently, but almost all feel it in some way. There is heavy drinking in Washington; there are many divorces; there are affairs with secretaries and constituents and lobbyists. Three male members of Congress have been arrested on morals charges in the past six years. (Republicans had worked hard for years to break the one-party domination of the Democrats in Mississippi, and at one point had elected two Republicans to Congress at the same time. But the "Great Drive" fizzled when one left to become a Senator and his successor was caught in a bathroom with another man conducting non-official business.)

I do not believe that politics attracts a lower class of people than other occupations or professions (in fact, there may be fewer boozers, playboys, and phonies per pound in the Congress than in corporate boardrooms), nor do I blame every moral failure within the hallowed halls of the Congress on the demands of the job; there are a great many things that happen in Washington that cannot be excused under the convenient cover of "stress". But the stress, the tensions, the destructive circumstances are heavy in Washington, heavy and pervasive, and few people escape unmarked. And the resulting problems—money problems, sex problems, drinking problems—create enormous opportunities for those who are looking for leverage and influence.

But for those who are truly concerned with congressional reform, or even with merely trying to understand such an awesome institution, such cases are more disturbing than they are instructive. *Direct* attempts to buy influence are already illegal and, as Abscam's victims learned, the laws are enforceable and the penalties are severe. So congressional reformers tend to concentrate their concern on *indirect* attempts to buy influence, through campaign contributions. Under current laws, however, individual contributors have very little influence on how a Congressman votes. No corporation may contribute anything at all to a candidate and no individual may contribute more than a thousand dollars to a single campaign. While that can add up (the totals could reach as much as $3,000 per individual in those rare cases where a candidate has three campaigns in a single year—a primary, a runoff primary, and a general election), those amounts simply aren't very decisive in a campaign that may cost half a million dollars or more. Even political action committees are limited to five thousand dollars per campaign.

To understand how the Congress works (and how to change how it works), it's important to realize that the biggest lobbying efforts are usually not by contributors or corporations but by a Congressman's own constituents, almost all of whom want to cut government spending by doing away with somebody else's projects while increasing the spending for their own.

This sort of misunderstanding of how the Congress works causes a lot of problems for organizations which have set out to change things. The nature of the Congress limits options and often forces Congressmen to choose between two extremes (too much of something or not enough). If reformers assume incorrectly that they know how the system works (if, for example, they assume that professional lobbyists exercise a great deal more evil influence than is the case), then the proposed solutions invariably go too far and their advocates lose credibility, when more temperate solutions, based on a clear understanding of the facts, might have won some support and done the country some good. This problem of petrified misconceptions is one reason that "reform" organizations like Common Cause and Ralph Nader's "Congress Watch" have lost so much of their influence in Congress.

I frankly haven't bothered to read all the amateur theories about what *really* happens inside the Congess. Walter Shapiro once reviewed some books about the Congress for the *Washington Post Magazine*. One, called *The Private World of Congress*, was written by two men, neither of whom had ever been a member of Congress.

One of the writers, David Fenno, claimed that members of Congress are motivated by three factors—the desire for re-election, the quest for power and prestige within the Congress, and a desire to write good laws. Another, David Mayhew, said that was nonsense: it's only the desire for re-election that determines what Congressmen do. Fenno may be close, though I wouldn't know how close without reading his book and I'm not that curious. Mayhew's theory, if Shapiro reports it accurately, is silly; I suspect that Mayhew is a political science professor.

Concern about re-election—a very real concern, with election campaigns only 13 or 14 months apart—is only occasionally an active force in determining what a Congressman does or how he votes. More often it is a *negative* factor, like an emergency brake ready to be pulled. A Congressman—perhaps it is here that we indulge in a bit of self-delusion—generally believes that he accurately reflects the thinking of most of his constituents on most issues. He therefore votes according to his own views as to what government is and what it should do, unless some indicator—a poll, for example, or a heavy surge of mail—signals that the folks back home might take exception. Then the fear of being defeated may work as a brake and cause the Congressman to vote differently than he would otherwise.

The difference is significant. If you assume that a Congressman's first concern is to be re-elected and that his votes are tailored to win the support of potential contributors, the way to prevent the control of the Congress by those who contribute large amounts to re-election campaigns is to limit even more severely what people can do to help a candidate. But if wealthy contributors are *not* calling the shots, and the problem is that Congressmen are doing their own thing, then the way to change the Congress is to encourage more public participation, financially and otherwise, not less—and to pay more attention to what a Congressman says and does when he's actually in Washington voting to spend your money to study the mating calls of toads or put a missile site in your backyard.

The problem is, most experts who presume to describe what the Congess is like, and thus how to change it, know very little about the Congress and how it works and thus find themselves lost like the proverbial pea in their own mental fog.

Most new members of Congress arrive in Washington full of high ideals and great ambitions. For some, perhaps, the ambitions are narrowly personal and selfish, but there are also in both parties men and women of great empathy, passion and outrage, who are sincerely eager to somehow make this a "better" world.

But time compresses and demands press in from every direction: hundreds, thousands, tens of thousands of letters to answer; scores of meetings to attend and speeches to give; thousands of votes to cast in every session, some on issues of great importance and many of practically no significance at all, each taking us from our offices to the House floor and back again in an interminable succession of round trips, eating hours out of every day to approve, unread, the contents of the previous day's *Congressional Record*, or to vote on issues which should never have occupied our attention in the first place—special favors for special interests, proclamations of this or declarations of that. And to top it all off, hordes of lobbyists and interest groups, some from our districts, many not, inviting us to receptions, breakfasts, luncheons, dinners, shows, parties, urging us to help them deplete bottomless supplies of liquor and food.

Mary Freeland, a young lady who was then dating a friend of mine, once gave me a copy of a short verse by Ed Seabough. The poem is certainly not a literary masterpiece in any sense, yet when I read the words—maybe it was my mood at the time, or the frustration I felt—I felt the same sort of sobering splash of cold water one receives on reading works like Yevtushenko's "Babi Yar" or Millay's "Renascence"— works that trigger questions that require answers.

> Where is the change I brought about?
> Where is the battle I helped to win?
> Where is the wrong that I made right?
> Where is the good that I have done?
> Where is the man I'd hoped to be?

Patrick Henry had a vision of a society in which men would be free from the tyranny of government. Martin Luther King, father and son, shared a dream of a society in which blacks would have the same rights and opportunities whites have. Susan B. Anthony, Elizabeth Cady Stanton and a hundred thousand others dreamed that women would have the rights and opportunities men have. Henry Ford had a far more utilitarian dream, but in a free society it created jobs for tens of thousands of men and women and gave the whole world greater mobility, more leisure, more productivity than ever before in history.

We in the Congress, more than most, have the opportunity to become the kind of people we would really like to be. There is power there, and a forum to speak from, and the ability to shape society. We must have our own dreams and give voice to them.

CHAPTER TWO:
THE POWER AND THE GLORY:
BECOMING A CONGRESSMAN

1. The Office Next to the Flushing Pipes

There are few thrills equal to setting foot on the House floor for the first time—and it's even more thrilling if it has cost you a massive personal debt, three years out of your life, and more than $600,000 in other people's money to get there.

It's probably inevitable, then, that the lessons begin early.

The Congress is very much a democratic place. Each representative draws the same salary, has the same number of votes, and has the same rights on the floor.

And yet as I sat there in the House chamber, waiting to be sworn in, I thought of my new office next to the bathroom (for nearly two years my private talks with visiting mayors and councilmen were to be punctuated by the sound of flushing pipes) and prepared for a long and noisy session.

Actually, pipes or not, it was a relief to have any office at all. And it wasn't much of one, because that day it still belonged to somebody else, Henry Nowak, a former county comptroller from Buffalo who was just finishing *his* term with the bathroom pipes and was getting ready to move on.

Unfortunately, Henry had either grown attached to the flushing or the moving process was stalled somewhere down the line. He–and his staff—were still in my office. The best I could do that day (and for a good many days afterwards) was to take my mother to see Henry Nowak's office. That was perhaps less thrilling for her than it would have been for Henry Nowak's mother.

I had been elected two months before, and since that time my staff and I had worked first out of our old campaign headquarters, then out of a cramped one-bedroom apartment in Oklahoma City. Now we were working out of half a dozen offices scattered around Capitol Hill.

My office was in my arms, pockets, folders, and briefcases.

I was sworn into office in January, 1977. But to the people of Oklahoma City I had become a Congressman—*their* Congressman—in November of 1976, the day after the election. On Tuesday I was one of five candidates; Wednesday morning the calls came—people with lost pension checks, people whose claims for disability benefits had been turned down or ignored, people looking for jobs, grants, favors. People complaining about things the Congress had done the year before and wanting to know why I hadn't put a stop to it.

It was useless and meaningless to explain that I would not take office for another two months, because government doesn't stop and the growth of government in the 20th century has spread its influence into so many lives that there is no time for transition. To the elderly widow whose lost social security check is the only source of income, to the disabled government worker who has not heard from an agency about his claim—and whose house payments are months overdue—an election only means that there is now some new avenue to try and no time for formalities.

I had no staff and no funds to hire one; no office and no funds to rent one; no money for equipment, no stamps for letters, no telephones.

We turned to the only source we had; the people who had worked in my campaign. For three years we had used their money and their time. Now we had to go back to them again, asking them to serve as a congressional staff without pay, offering whatever help we could and trying very hard not to usurp the prerogatives of the *real* Congressman while I began to assemble a staff and arrange for the move to Washington.

I *do* think I was confident I would win, but I suppose my confidence wasn't all it might have been. One of the other candidates had planned his move well in advance; months before the election he and his wife announced they were scouting around in Maine for a "vacation home" to use when the Congress was not in session. I suppose they found a place. Unfortunately, he was eliminated in the primaries. I don't know whether he ever got to use the house in Maine or not.

There is something to be said, however, for having enough confidence to do *some* planning. My wife and I did find a place to live in the

Washington suburbs, but the arrangements left a little to be desired. Weeks after we had signed a rental agreement—and while I lived in luxury at one of the swank hotels near Dulles airport, receiving party-sponsored lessons on how to run a congressional office (and get re-elected)—my wife was in a crowded room at a nearby Holiday Inn with my mother, two daughters, half a dozen suitcases and two dogs, waiting for the furniture to arrive and our new home's occupants to leave.

Meanwhile, I was becoming acquainted with the other "freshmen" Republicans. "Freshman" members of Congress have even less in common than freshmen in a college fraternity. There was a tremendous age disparity—Eldon Rudd, a former FBI agent and a county supervisor in Phoenix, was then 56; Dan Quayle, a small-town publisher from Indiana, was 29. And there was a difference in experience as well. Bob Badham had been in the California state legislature for 14 years; Carl Pursell had been a state senator in Michigan; I had never run for anything before and didn't know a quorum from a kumquat.

Our backgrounds were different. Ron Marlenee was a rancher in Montana; Dan Marriott was an ordained Mormon clergyman. And though we were all Republicans, our philosophies varied widely, from Bob Dornan, of California, on the right, to Iowa's Jim Leach, who was somewhere in the middle, and Bruce Caputo of New York, Newt Steers, of Maryland, and "Cappy" Hollenbeck, of New Jersey, who were our class liberals. (Leach later moved to the left, Caputo moved to the right and Steers was moved out of Congress—the only member of the Class of 1978 to be defeated for re-election.) In addition to our natural differences, there was another factor: we each represented somebody else—our constituents—and they were as different as a political map of America. Badham, for example, had been elected in a district so heavily Republican that to win the primary was to win the election; three out of four voters in *my* district were Democrats.

Those early days at the hotel didn't help much, I only remember one "lesson", a staff management session in which we were warned to "keep the monkey—paperwork and minor decisions—on somebody's else's back." It made sense, of course; that's what staff assistants are for, and using them properly helps a Congressman give full attention to major things. But for most of us it doesn't work that way. There are no subordinates to whom you can readily pass the blame in a congressional office: a Congressman's constituents will hold him personally responsible when letters aren't answered, when replies are rude, when meetings fall through, and many Congressmen are often forced in self defense to involve themselves in the most minute details of the office operation—a fact which greatly increases frustration and reduces effectiveness.

At any rate, having made the move to Washington, with my wife, mother, children and dogs in a hotel room, the furniture in a truck, somebody else in our house, somebody else in my office, another month before the first paycheck, a brief acquaintance with one-twentieth of the House, and instructions to "let somebody else do it", I was ready to be a Congressman.

2. Committee Assignments: Chefs in the Motor Pool

Two rather awesome discoveries still dominate my memory of those first mind-boggling days as a member of Congress:

• the amazing, and rather curious, process by which the Republican leadership made critical decisions about committee assignments that were to have a far-reaching impact on federal law (and, in one instance, on the entire national energy policy), and

• a cigar-smoking California liberal named Phillip Burton, my first "enemy" in the Congress.

It is said that a chef who joins the army will be assigned to the motor pool and a mechanic will become the general's secretary. But there has been more design—and therefore less excuse—in the fact that Republicans so often assign their best craftsmen to the kitchen and their best chefs to the garage.

A select group of senior Republican Congressmen, known collectively as the Executive Committee of the Committee on Committees of the House Republican Conference (TECOTCOCOTHRC), determines which Republican members of Congress will sit on which committees—easily the most important career decision ever made by or for any Member of Congress, since most of the work of the House is done in committee and those initial committee assignments, made within days or weeks after a Member's first election, may well frame that Congressman's entire public career—his participation, his influence, the issues he deals with and becomes knowledgeable about.

The procedure has since been improved, but in my first term it cost us dearly.

The Executive Committee (TECOTCOCOTHRC) was made up of one Congressman (the senior member) from each of the states with large numbers of Republican Congressmen. (In 1977, for example,

New York had 11 Republican Congressmen; its representative, Frank Horton, had 11 votes. California had 14; its representative, Bob Wilson, had 14 votes.)

By contrast, there were 42 Republican Congressmen from states which had each elected only one or two Republicans to the House; those 42 Congressmen, combined, had a total of two members on the Executive Committee which determined committee assignments—one chosen to represent all those Members from those states which had only one Republican Congressman, another from those states which had two. Each had only one vote on the executive committee, whether representing one member or 20).

The results were surprisingly predictable. The so-called big states (in terms of Republican strength) would get together informally and form coalitions to divide up seats on the powerful committees. If the Pennsylvania members felt it was their turn for a seat on Ways and Means, and if the Michigan members felt it was their turn to place somebody on Appropriations, it was simple enough for such arrangements to be worked out—all of California's 14 votes lumped with all of Michigan's eight. Work Ohio or Illinois into the deal over lunch, or by phone, and things were set.

To be fair, there were sometimes significant exceptions. Some members of Congress so clearly stand out for their diligence or ability that they eventually receive choice spots no matter where they start from (meaning, no matter what *state* they come from).

And there were times when the system worked well, and when the choices could not be improved upon, no matter *how* the selections were made. Two examples come to mind: John Rousselot, a feisty, creative, and outrageously funny Californian, who was selected to serve on the Ways and Means Committee when another Californian, Bill Ketchum, died, and David Stockman, who, as a freshman, took "the Michigan seat" on the powerful Interstate and Foreign Commerce Committee and became one of the most highly respected—and most articulate—Republicans in the House (and, later, President Reagan's budget director).

But there is sometimes a high price to pay for such a process.

In January, 1977, two members of my "freshman class" were appointed to the Interstate and Foreign Commerce Committee—Stockman and Pennsylvania's Marc Marks, a slight, white-haired loner who worried constantly about re-election and quickly emerged as one of the most liberal members of Congress in either party.

There are not many issues on which all Republicans agree, but there are some on which *most* agree, and one of them, that year, was the need to remove excessive federal regulation of natural gas prices in order to stimulate increased exploration and production. That view was pretty well accepted by Republicans in the Congress, and removal of controls—deregulation—had become a key part of the party's energy platform.

In 1978 the Committee on Interstate and Foreign Commerce considered a proposal to deregulate natural gas prices, and although the Democrats then held an overwhelming majority on the committee—better than two to one—this Republican program came within a single vote of being approved by the committee and reported favorably to the full House for passage. That one vote—the only Republican vote against the Republican position—was cast by Marc Marks.

I do not intend to suggest—or even hint—that Marc Marks should have voted any other way if he believed that deregulation was wrong. Marc's name—his full name—is Marc *Lincoln* Marks. Marc retired in 1982, but while he was in Congress he signed his letters, issued his press releases, thought of himself as Marc Lincoln Marks. He voted the way he thought was right; could *you* have asked him to do otherwise?

The blame (from a Republican viewpoint) was not his: it belonged to the amazing system by which Republicans then selected who would serve on which committees. The Republican Party had shot down a key part of its own platform, retained federal controls as a principal element in the nation's energy policy, and increased America's energy dependence on foreign sources by its curious insistence that the big states had the right to divide up choice committee assignments among themselves—even though party leaders were well aware that the deregulation issue would be decided in the Commerce committee that year.

It has been suggested that if the Republican Party ever decides to form a firing squad, it will probably do so in a circle. This was a good example.

Things *have* changed, however. For several years a number of Republican Congressmen from the smaller states had been trying, unsuccessfully, to change the committee assignment system. Their efforts failed for a simple reason: the decision to approve the process, and the membership of TECOTCOCOTHRC for the forthcoming Congress, was made at a meeting of the Republican Conference (all House Republicans) before the session actually began—and before committee assignments were made. New members were understandably reluctant to participate in a challenge to party elders who, if the challenge failed, would be determining *their* committee assignments. (Even if the challenge succeeded, in fact, the same senior members would continue to have an enormous amount of influence over the decisions). In 1979, however, Arlan Stangeland, a stubborn Scandinavian farmer from Minnesota, decided to try again, at a special meeting of the Republican Conference held *after* the session had started and committee assignments had been made. For weeks Arlan cornered other members and lined up votes. As a result, the Conference agreed to make the process more equitable, although Congressmen from the so-called "big" states still have a substantial advantage. Perhaps Republican legislative suicides will be less frequent in the future.

Equity, however, does not necessarily mean an end to frustration.

Early in my second term, Dave Treen, a Republican member of the Armed Services Committee, was elected governor of Louisiana (no small accomplishment in a state in which Democrats outnumber Republicans by something like ten to one). The campaign he waged to win that office may have been even more intense than the one that was later waged in the Congress by members who wanted to move into the committee position he was vacating.

Treen's election, in a state Republicans had lost to Jimmy Carter four years before, was a tremendous boost, and a principal source of conversation in the Republican cloakroom for the better part of a day—a rare impact indeed. At the same time, a number of Republican members had become somewhat eager for Dave to move on; Treen was popular enough, but it is here as it is elsewhere; others were already beginning to cast covetous eyes on the vacancy his resignation would create on the Armed Services Committee, much like the child who learns a brother is missing and asks the most important question first: "Can I have his room?"

It was well into the evening, several days later, when Susan Bingham came into my office. Susan is now Susan Bingham-Neal, the wife of a top White House official and, in her own right, an effective lobbyist for a business federation, but she was then my administrative assistant, the principal member of the staff, as her husband, Rick, had been before her. Susan is bright, bubbly, lively, and was an extremely popular manager of the 21 diverse personalities who served in our one office in Washington and six offices in Oklahoma City. But she was perceptive as well, with a natural political instinct, and although she had not lived in the district (she's from Tulsa), I had developed a routine of going through the day's activities with her—important mail, phone calls, political stirrings, as well as committee work, staff assignments and emerging issues.

This night she took from her stack of papers a letter that might otherwise have been filed or trashed, a routine notice of a pending committee vacancy, and suggested I might want to consider it. It was a letter from John Rhodes, then the House Minority Leader (this was before Republicans, in a feisty mood after the Reagan election, began calling themselves "Republicans," instead of "the Minority"), inviting applications from anybody interested in the vacancy on Armed Services. It was late—well past eight o'clock—and I stuffed the letter into a briefcase along with other paperwork I was taking home. (I almost always carry home at least one stuffed briefcase; sometimes I carry the same papers back to work the next morning without the slightest disturbance.)

On the way home, my thoughts kept coming back to the letter from Rhodes. Once there, I walked into the small office I had set up in the basement and read the letter again and again.

The possibility was tempting.

I had long been seriously—and increasingly—concerned about the deterioration of the nation's defense capability, and had taken a leading role in warning about the growing Soviet lead in manpower and weapons production. A few months before I had touched heavily on my fears in a lecture at a foreign policy seminar sponsored by the Center for Constructive Alternatives at Hillsdale College, in Michigan. Only a few days before Treen's election I had taken the lead in an hour-long presentation on the House floor about the Soviet Union's potential control of the world's principal sea lanes.

But, as Susan had immediately recognized, the economic aspects of the defense program were important, too—especially in Oklahoma. Tinker Air Force Base in my district was, and is, the largest employer in the state. There are three other military installations in Oklahoma—an important army post at Lawton and air force bases at Enid and Altus—yet none of Oklahoma's Congressmen then served on the Armed Services Committee. (One, Tom Steed, had a seat on the Appropriations Committee, which gave him a key vantage point, but Tom was past 75 and in poor health, and would not seek re-election.)

There was an obvious risk involved in seeking the change. All of us attempt to put as good a face as possible on our committee assignments so our constituents will feel that we have moved into positions from which we can do something "of benefit to the district"—an unfortunate side effect of the tendency for community leaders to want a Congressman who can somehow bring home the bacon.

By seeking to change committee assignments a Congressman is revealing to his constituents that he has less than the best committee assignments in the Congress, a fact nobody likes to admit (it is constantly amazing to hear freshmen attempt to explain to constituents in Iowa or Montana the importance of the Committee on the District of Columbia). And, in the event he is *not* selected he runs the additional risk of conveying to his constituents that he is not influential with the important people in his own party. I avoided the problem by simply not telling very many people that I was trying to switch. If I lost, nobody would ever know; if I won, it would prove my prestige and influence in the Congress since I would have apparently been selected with no effort on my part.

I put the letter down and called Susan. The next day I placed a call to Rhodes.

I had angered Rhodes and other Republican leaders when, in early 1977, young, impatient, impetuous, I had addressed the national Young Republican convention in Memphis and bluntly criticized the Republican leadership in the House for lack of imagination and lack of aggressiveness. (John Rhodes seemed to have lost some of his combativeness as a result of a quarter-century as part of a minority party with no control over events in the House. It often appeared that he had simply become accustomed to being without power. Nor can he be faulted for his failed spirit after so many years of dashed hopes. As Vera Pavlona says in Chernyshevsky's novel, "What Is To Be Done?", "They deplore the present, but they believe in its eternity, or little short of it.")

Copies of my speech were circulated among Republicans on the House floor almost before I had returned from Tennessee, and for days afterwards Republican members of Congress came to me on the floor, in the cloakroom, in my office, confessing that they, too, had been disturbed by a lack of effectiveness in the party's leadership.

Furious, Rhodes confronted me on the House floor and made it clear that one could not expect to make such comments with impunity.

A short time later House Speaker Tip O'Neill had announced formation of a select Energy Committee. My constituents included literally hundreds of small, independent producers whose livelihoods rode on the risks of oil and gas exploration. I knew there was little likelihood that Rhodes would recommend me for a seat on the committee after our confrontation, so I set out to win the position on my own.

O'Neill had determined that he would fill the special committee by selecting members from each standing House Committee which had jurisdiction over energy legislation. In addition he would appoint a small number of members selected by the leadership (O'Neill for the Democrats and Rhodes for the Republicans). Since that last possibility was undoubtedly foreclosed in my case, I zeroed in on the one Republican seat to be filled from the House Interior Committee—on which I was the lowest-ranking member.

There were two obvious hurdles which had to be overcome. The top-ranking Republican on the full committee, who would obviously have the assignment if he wanted it, was Joe Skubitz, a short, rumpled, veteran Kansas Congressman already eyeing retirement. The ranking member of the Energy subcommittee was Maryland's Bob Bauman, an aggressive conservative partisan who might be expected to want the seat on the committee for the unique opportunity it would offer for a direct philosophical confrontation over the direction of the nation's future energy policy.

I approached both Skubitz and Bauman directly and stated my case: There were few congressional districts more involved in energy production than my own, I told them, and thus few members of the House with comparable ability to draw on constituents who had expertise in energy production but were not tied to the so-called "Seven Sisters," the major international oil companies.

After several conversations, both Skubitz and Bauman agreed to step aside. Skubitz asked only one thing: assurance that I agreed with him on the basic priorities of a national energy policy (increased production first and conservation second, rather than the other way around). Bauman asked nothing, but he undoubtedly remembered that soon after I joined the committee he had challenged a more senior member, Michigan's Phil Ruppe, for the top position of the Energy committee. Such challenges are rare, and successful ones even more so, yet Bauman had won, largely because other Republicans on the subcommittee feared that the likeable, easy-going Ruppe would not be able to stand up to the chairman, Mo Udall, and partly because of a fear that in many cases the environmentally liberal Ruppe might be closer to Udall's position than that of his Republican colleagues. I had supported Bauman's challenge and, while it was never mentioned, that vote might have added to Bauman's willingness to help me this time.

Both Skubitz and Bauman warned, however, that at least one senior member of the committee, Alaska's Don Young, had said *he* wanted that spot on the new committee.

I set Young's name aside and began to call on the other members of the committee, all of whom outranked me in seniority (even my fellow freshmen, Eldon Rudd, of Arizona, Dan Mariott, of Utah, and Ron Marlenee, of Montana, all outranked me by luck of the draw, which had determined relative rankings of members with equal seniority). All agreed to let me have the position, some as a favor, some because of the nature of my district, and my familiarity with energy issues, and others, frankly, because they were more interested in public lands issues or environmental concerns than with the committee's energy aspects.

Finally, I went to see Don Young. Don, did indeed want the position. Alaska is one of the nation's great repositories of energy supplies, and Alaska's future economic growth is largely tied to the development of energy resources. Yet an important and delicate balance had to be struck, because Alaska is also a last frontier of great natural beauty, and Alaskans, including Young, live in fear of seeing the land despoiled.

The House was then preparing to debate the Alaskan Lands Bill, which would have set aside millions of acres of Alaska for environmental protection. Young and other Alaska officials wanted the protection, but also wanted to carve out a few promising sections of the state for possible mineral and energy exploration. Young was eager to have the time to work on the Alaskan Lands Bill, but also wanted to make sure Alaska's substantial economic and environmental interests would be protected in the workings of the new committee.

Because the assignment was now clearly his if he wanted it, he was also fearful that if he allowed somebody else to get the position it might look to Alaskans as though he had been bypassed for the job.

We came to an agreement. I had already publicly supported Young's position on the Alaskan Lands Bill, so Don agreed to step aside if I would agree to watch out for Alaska's interests on the select committee and if I would give him a letter making it clear that he could have had the assignment, and that I was committed to preserving the important balance Alaskans wanted. It had taken several meetings, in committee, on the floor, and in Young's office, to work out the ar-

rangement. I had won the committee assignment. Don had won a vocal supporter in a key position.

After we had agreed, I returned to Skubitz and he informed Rhodes
that I was the choice of the Interior Committee's Republicans for the
seat on the Energy Committee.

Two years later, seeking the seat on the Armed Services Committee, I knew I could take no consolation in having been formally appointed by Rhodes to the Energy committee. Although Rhodes made
the official appointment, others had made the selection. I remembered
his angry threat on the House floor after the Memphis speech and I entered his office with little hope that I could win his support.

Things had changed, however. Rhodes had responded to increasing
pressure from other Republicans who had begun to echo my concerns,
who had even begun to talk openly of dumping Rhodes as minority
leader. Now, stimulated by the influx of energetic, creative, younger
Republicans who had first been elected in 1976 and 1978, Rhodes was
showing a greater willingness to carry the fight to the Democrats, and
was, in fact, finishing the 96th Congress with a series of bold challenges which greatly helped Republicans across the country who were
preparing for the 1980 elections.

In addition, I had taken on a number of tasks which did not go unnoticed by the Republican leadership, including serving as director of
an intensive month-long national campaign to focus public attention
on the responsibility of House Democrats for continual increases in individual income taxes for more than a quarter of a century.

To my surprise, Rhodes seemed friendly and encouraging, although
he gave no commitment and repeatedly pointed out that in any case
the assignment was not his to give. Nonetheless, I left his office in a
more hopeful mood than when I went in.

I began to map out my campaign.

The principal competition was to come from Bob Dornan—
intense, flamboyant, excitable, a perpetual-motion Californian with a
nearly encyclopedic knowledge of defense issues—and four first-term
Congressmen, Bob Davis, of Michigan, and Gerry Solomon, of New
York (both of whom, like Dornan, came from states with large numbers
of votes on the selection committee), Ken Kramer, of Colorado, and
Larry Hopkins, of Kentucky, who came into the contest with considerable early strength because, under the revised selection procedure, the
combined votes of the states which had three Republican Congressmen would be cast by Dr. Tim Lee Carter, another Kentuckian, who
had taken Hopkins under his wing.

As a first step, I mailed a detailed three-page letter to Rhodes and the 14 members of the executive committee, recounting my past involvement in defense issues, describing my other reasons for seeking the position and simply describing the state of Oklahoma.

I had found at the beginning of the 96th Congress, when I first attempted to leave the Interior Committee, that members of the executive committee were glaringly ignorant about the nature of the district I represented and believed I already had the best committee assignment in the House. As a result, they had simply passed over my request and had concentrated instead on members who had not yet had such good fortune.

Because I am from Oklahoma, there was a widespread belief that I represented vast unpopulated areas of land, and thus had a deep interest in such issues as public land management, national parks, mining, water power and other major ingredients of the Interior Committee's jurisdiction. Indeed, it is precisely those issues that make Interior an extremely popular committee assignment for most Congressmen from Western states. But my district then (before the 1982 redistricting) was compact and urban: while other members of Interior represented vast acreages of forest or rangeland, I represented a district of skyscrapers, expressways, factories, shopping centers, suburban blue-collar workers, inner-city blacks and business executives.

Clearly if there was any blame to be attached for this misunderstanding it was entirely my own. There are no official briefing sheets prepared for the selection committee and what the members know or don't know is entirely up to the applicants for committee positions. Like other members of Congress, I was unaware of the details of most other congressional districts, or of district boundaries, and it was not surprising, therefore, that Congressmen from New York, Illinois, California, or Kentucky might not know much more about my constituency that the basic fact that I represent Oklahoma—with whatever images that might arouse.

Now I was again asking to leave Interior, this time for the seat on Armed Services, and I was going to make it clear this time that Interior's interminable debates about copper mines in Utah and battlefield parks in Virginia were not, in fact, the concerns that kept me awake at night.

Actually, I could have given up my other committee assignment instead, but the political power of the labor unions makes it difficult for the Republican leadership to find members willing to serve on the Education and Labor Committee, where confrontations with organized labor are inevitable. Therefore, I had to promise Rhodes that if I won the seat on Armed Services I would make up for it my keeping my seat on Education and Labor as well.

Next, I found a campaign manager, a "champion" within the executive committee who could advise me and argue in my behalf. I went to Manuel Lujan, of New Mexico, who represented the states on the executive committee which had a single Republican Congressman. Manny is a slight, quiet, easy-going man with a reputation as a steady, competent legislator. He is, without question, one of the most popular and least controversial members of the House. Then, with Lujan helping to map strategy, I turned to friends outside the Congress.

The first to respond was Tom Stafford, an Air Force general, former astronaut, a personal friend for nearly 10 years (we had met in 1970 when he was still a colonel, recently back from space, and exploring a Senate race against an increasingly unpopular Fred Harris, and I was one of the three members of that unofficial and short-lived campaign's somewhat informal steering committee. Though he later went back to the space program instead, as a general and commander of the first joint U.S.-Soviet space mission, we had remained friends). Now Tom helped me as I had helped him so many years before, with letters and phone calls to senior Republicans.

Soon others joined him: Admiral Thomas Moorer, a former chairman of the Joint Chiefs of Staff; Admiral Mark Hill, former Deputy Chief of Naval Operations; Admiral John McCain, former commander of the U.S. fleet in the Pacific; General Daniel Graham, former director of the Defense Intelligence Agency—all wrote urging members of the executive committee to put me in a position to help in the rebuilding of the nation's defense capabilities.

Next, I turned to a round of personal visits, beginning with the senior member of the executive committee, California's Bob Wilson, who was also the top-ranking Republican member of the Armed Services Committee. We met in Wilson's spacious office in the Rayburn Building. The walls, bookshelves, tables, and Wilson's desk were cluttered with eagles and elephants—the traditional collections of partisan Republicans.

Wilson, to my surprise, said he did not think California had any claim on the seat since there were already two other Californians on the committee, and indicated he would not be actively supporting Dornan's candidacy. I was encouraged; if I could pick up Wilson's support, I knew I would have a much better chance of making it past the early eliminations. Wilson then surprised me again by saying the race seemed to have come down to a contest between Kramer and me. He was surprised to learn that Kramer was still a first-term member—a shocking reminder that as sessions run together, and members continue to have only limited contact with those on other committees, the degree of knowledge we have about each other is sometimes very slight. As a more senior member, he said, I would probably have priority in a race between myself and a first-term Congressman. Another reason for optimism: except for Dornan and myself, everybody who had expressed interest in the Armed Services seat was a "freshman."

I left the meeting with hopes high and set up a meeting with New York's Frank Horton. Again, the meeting went well—and again I was surprised to find the degree to which more senior members were uninformed about the younger members, including how long they had served and what kinds of districts they represented. Although Horton was apparently locked in by the candidacy of Gerry Solomon, a Marine Corps veteran, Solomon was not campaigning aggressively and no longer appeared likely to be a major contender (in fact, he withdrew before the committee met).

Other meetings took place in a variety of settings—on the House floor, in the cloakroom, wherever I could corner the people who would be making the decision.

My immediate problem was simple: the tedious selection process called for a continuing series of ballots, with the bottom man dropped from the list after each vote. I somehow had to win enough votes in the early balloting to avoid being eliminated before committee members who had their own candidates in the race would be free to vote for me.

Then, as the time for the selection drew near, I received a disturbing tip. Several members of the committee were leaning toward other contenders because I "didn't need" the position.

Traditionally, Republican committee assignments have been made with only passing regard to an applicant's background or ability to be effective in the committee's work. There are two criteria which outweigh all others: does one of the larger states have a claim to the seat (is it, for example, Ohio's "turn"?); does one of the candidates "need" the position in order to be re-elected? If the assignment would give a boost to a troubled incumbent by giving him added prestige in his district, this would take precedence over applications by members who seemed to be in good shape back home.

I quickly prepared another (and, in retrospect, absolutely amazing) letter to the members of the selection committee: after having worked seven days a week to stay in touch with my constituents, returning to the congressional district almost every weekend and during every recess (a schedule that would ultimately cause me to lose my wife and family), and having done what my constituents apparently considered to be a good job, I had been rewarded by receiving 80 percent of the vote when I ran for re-election in 1978, carrying every precinct in the congressional district and carrying every segment of the electorate— Republicans, Democrats, Independents, blue-collar workers, union members, executives, blacks—everybody.

Now, as I tried to move into a position where I could be more effective in doing something about one of the greatest concerns of the people who had so overwhelmingly re-elected me, I found that the great support I had received was a handicap. If I had won by only a few votes—one, perhaps—it would be clear that I needed the more prestigious committee position. But 80 percent? I was caught in a Republican "Catch 22." To get into a position to be effective in an area in which I had a vital interest, I had to do such a poor job in Congress that my constituents were on the verge of tossing me out.

I prepared a careful letter spelling out the hard facts of life of representing a district in the southwestern United States. I was the first Republican elected to Congress from my district since 1928; three-fourths of the voters in my district are Democrats, and so forth.

As I wrote the letter, I steamed with anger. I was proud of the work I had done, proud of the victory I had won, and now I was having to "explain away" that victory, belittle it, and pretend it was an accident. I sent the letter, but I regret sending it and would never do it again.

Finally, the committee met. Hours passed but I heard no word. I called John Rhodes. He told me it had been a close contest, a real cliff-hanger that lasted through ballot after ballot, as the other eight or nine contenders were eliminated. Finally, he said, in a very close vote, the committee had selected Larry Hopkins.

I was stunned. Larry Hopkins is a competent congressmen, but had until that time shown little visible interest in national defense issues.

Slowly I began to piece the picture together. Rhodes had, in fact, been helpful in the committee's discussions (although John Ashbrook, a colleague on the Education and Labor Committee, later told me he had heard another committee member, a senior member of the party's leadership, complain about my gall in criticizing Rhodes and the party's leadership two years before). Finally, Doc Carter, in poor health and preparing to retire, had made an emotional plea for Hopkins, who had won with only 51 percent of the vote in a heavily Democratic district. Hopkins, he said, needed the job in order to get re-elected. (Hopkins had let it be known, as part of his campaign, that if the executive committee would grant him the seat on Armed Services for the remainder of the session he would not insist on remaining on the committee in the next Congress.)

Hopkins will undoubtedly do a good job. The circumstances of his selection continue to bother me, though, and for much the same reasons that I was disturbed by the selection of Marc Marks to serve on the Commerce Committee.

The Congress is not a stadium; writing laws that affect the daily lives of a quarter of a billion people is no game. A serious political party should be in the business of carefully placing its people where they can have the greatest impact. Committee selections should take into account a member's background and expertise, and the needs and interests of the people he represents, not the size of his state's Republican delegation in the Congress, or how much he may need help in the next election, unless all other important considerations are somewhat equal.

3. Udall and Burton: Alice in Wonderland and the Heart of Darkness

As for my own personal baptism into committee politics: I met Phillip Burton for the first time within days after I was sworn in.

Phil Burton, who died suddenly in April, 1983, during a trip to his California district, was one of the most interesting Members of Congress—a throwback to the old-fashioned politics of the smoke-filled room. Perhaps the most strikingly activist liberal in the House (but always behind the scenes; he rarely spoke on the House floor), Phil Burton looked tough as nails. But looks can be deceiving; they don't make nails that tough.

A former leader of the powerful left-wing Democratic Study Group, then chairman of the Democratic Steering Committee, Burton, when I met him, had just lost a fight for majority leader, by one vote, after leading on the first two ballots.

We met in a meeting of the House Interior Committee. Mo Udall was the committee's chairman; Burton ranked second, and acted as sort of majority leader in the committee, causing me for a time to have the mistaken impression that Burton was dominating the committee (I came to realize that the courtly and soft-spoken Udall was very much in charge, but that was later; at the moment Burton seemed to tower over the meeting, offering resolutions, interrupting, cutting off debate, moving for votes).

As for me, I was the lowest-ranking member of the committee, even among the Republicans.

At one point in the proceedings, however, I was moved to speak against one of Burton's many proposals, which it seemed to me were stacking an already-stacked committee even more. We were setting up committee rules and the issue was procedural, a dispute over the use of proxies, perhaps, or the need for a quorum. The procedure was new to me, as were the issues. I picked up one of the notepads that had been placed in front of each committee member, carefully wrote out some remarks criticizing Burton's many proposals, raised my hand and was recognized (although Joe Skubitz had to whisper to Udall to tell him who I was).

I read my short statement. When I was finished, Burton, who had been listening intently, peered at me over his half-glasses. "I see that our new member wrote out his little speech," he said. "Perhaps he's planning to have it published."

I was embarrassed and angry. It was my first day in the committee, my first confrontation with one of the "enemy" leaders, and I had been embarrassed in front of not only my Republican colleagues but also—and worse—in front of the Democrats. (It surprised me then, and still does, to realize that the people in the "audience" simply don't enter into it; from the first day you're simply not aware that they're there.)

I knew I wasn't going to be loved by the liberals in the House, but I had every intention of being respected by them. Being humiliated the first day wasn't the way to earn that respect.

I regained the floor (although I had to ask a staff member how to do it).

"Mr. Burton made a comment about my 'prepared speech'," I said. "Well, it *was* prepared, and if he'd like to read it I'll be glad to put it in the Record. I'll even be glad to take it to his office so he can read it again."

The room became absolutely still. I honestly thought the cigar was going to fall from Burton's mouth. I think Udall thought it was funny;

I know Burton didn't. He was furious. For weeks—for months—he was cold and hostile.

Republicans on the committee told me afterwards that Burton had been testing me; he liked to pick on a new member to see how far he can go, to see whether you'll take it or stand your ground. Later, when Burton began to come up to me on the floor, drape his huge arm around my shoulder and begin some small talk or tell a joke or discuss a bill coming up in the committee, those same friends told me I had won Phil Burton's respect. "Not very many freshmen would have stood up to him like that," they said. "It made him mad, but he has to respect you."

Phil Burton was a unique member of Congress. There is no other Congressman I'd have hated more to have as an enemy. But he was also a surprisingly good friend at times, especially to those who had known him for a long time. Bill Ketchum had served with Burton in the California legislature before both came to Congress and when Ketchum died of a heart attack during my first term, Phil Burton rose on the House floor to mourn the loss of his old friend. In the middle of his speech, Burton burst into tears. Ketchum, a Republican, was as conservative as Burton was liberal, but if Phil Burton said he loved Bill Ketchum, I believe it.

As it turned out, that run-in with Phil Burton, in a committee where the chairman didn't even know my name, was one of the *better* things that happened to me in those early days.

The Interior and Insular Affairs Committee, with its Phil Burton, its Mo Udall, its John Seiberling (John's family made a fortune in free enterprise and he is apparently trying to atone for it by changing the system so nobody else will suffer the same fate)—*that* committee as I found out, is just the *outskirts* of the enemy camp. It gets darker as you go deeper.

The other committee I was assigned to, the Committee on Education and Labor, made me think of that song, "Please, Mister Custer, I don't wanna go." Being on Interior is a lot like being with Alice in Wonderland; this—this was Conrad's heart of darkness.

Phil Burton was on this committee, too, which should have told me something, but he was less powerful here.

There were three principal and overpowering personalities on the Education and Labor Committee when I served on it—the chairman, Carl Perkins, of Kentucky; the leader (at least on most labor issues), Frank Thompson, of New Jersey; and Bill Ford, of Michigan, the committee version of George Raft. They were the boss, the mouthpiece and the enforcer. Together, they were awesome.

Being a Republican on that committee was a lot like being a peanut on a railroad track; your only choice was whether you ended up in large chunks or small.

All House committees had the same ratios—roughly two Democrats to one Republican—and on almost every committee there were, among those Democrats, a number who were practically indistinguishable from Republicans, conservative Democrats from the South and Southwest who often vote with Republicans on major issues. But Carl Perkins likes to keep things simple, and on the Education and Labor Committee there's no such nonsense. It's a political science professor's dream: the divisions are clear, obvious and as predictable as a Woody Hayes football team (nothing fancy, just the tanks). On occasion, a Republican will vote with the Democrats (I was one of the sponsors of a higher education bill that came out of the committee, and was passed in the House, for example), but Democrats on that committee vote for a Republican amendment, or against a committee bill, about as often as it snows coconuts in Cancun.

Good amendments and bad amendments all got approximately the same treatment:

Perkins would listen indulgently, a tolerant, long-suffering smile on his face; Thompson would drop a bit of sarcasm on the thing; Ford (the hit man) would attack it; New York's Ted Weiss would be vaguely offended by what it would all mean to New York; Paul Simon, of Illinois, would show great understanding, always implying a general sort of agreement with the amendment's intent—and then the Republicans would vote for the amendment and the Democrats would vote against it.

Unlike Interior's Udall, who is something of a master at producing the exact number of proxies he needs, Perkins and Thompson would seldom throw in proxy votes for absent members because they rarely needed the votes (when they did need proxies, it was only because some of the Democrats didn't bother to come to the meetings. I imagine it *did* get boring.)

For obvious reasons, there have been years when the Republican leadership has had to draft people to serve on Education and Labor. When they get on, they can't wait to get off. At the end of my first term, so many Republicans left the committee that I shot up to sixth in seniority and became the top-ranking Republican member of one of the committee's subcommittees.

The ranking Democrat on a committee is the chairman; if there is ever a Republican majority, the ranking Republican will become chairman. The two "ranking" positions—Democrat and Republican—are roughly equal; the chairman—the "ranking" Democrat—determines when meetings will be held, what bills will be considered, who will testify, whether the bill will be advanced to "markup" (a rewriting session in preparation for taking the bill to the floor) and other such matters. The "ranking" Republican determines whether he can make it to the meetings on time, what suit to wear to the hearings and what questions to ask of the witnesses the chairman invited. It's a matter of shared responsibility.

(The system *can* work differently, although the chairman retains the power to make it work this way, and the burden for making it work differently falls entirely on the Republican. Many committee and subcommittee chairmen do run their committees exactly this way, retaining all power and making all decisions unilaterally in keeping with the Speaker's general belief that the minority party has only one function in government, and that's to help make up a quorum.)

I was the senior Republican on the Health and Safety Subcommittee, however, and the chairman was, and is, a man named Joseph Gaydos, an unassuming Pennsylvania steel-town lawyer. Gaydos, like most Pennsylvania Democrats, is somewhat partisan, but he can't help being a bit like an ethnic Archie Bunker without the prejudice—a robust, stocky guy who ought to be downing beers and singing off-key in a small-town tavern with the last grimy shift from the coal mine or steel mill. It's very hard not to like him.

Of course, I worked at creating a good relationship with Gaydos. Congressional committees often take extended field trips (junkets) to exotic, far-off places—long periods of travel together in which members of the committee can get to know each other on a more relaxed basis and improve their ability to work together when they get back. I decided I would force myself to go along on those trips so I could get to know Gaydos and the more active subcommittee Democrats like Don Bailey, a former Michigan lineman who played in the Rose Bowl once, and Ozzie Myers, a former cargo checker on the Philadelphia waterfront who was later convicted in the Abscam scandal and expelled from Congress.

I soon began to suspect that I had chosen the wrong committee. Our exotic trips were to Philadelphia, Springfield, Missouri, and Jersey City. I skipped the last one; there are *some* sacrifices I'm not willing to make.

CHAPTER THREE
THE TASTE OF VICTORY, THE TASTE OF DEFEAT

1. Common Situs: the Unions Lose a Big One

The Education and Labor Committee is, for most Republicans, a lot like the first circle of Dante's inferno—pleasant enough if you're willing to accept the fact that it's meaningless and you're probably not going anywhere.

Ironically, overwhelming labor-union domination of the Education and Labor Committee has been a principal cause of the growing number of union defeats on the House floor in recent years.

Coming off two-to-one party-line victories in subcommittee and committee, Perkins, Thompson, and Ford would arrive on the House floor like football coaches who have played Podunk U for six weeks and then go up against Bear Bryant. They overestimate their own strength and underestimate the opposition.

The Education and Labor Committee is so unbalanced, so out of sync even with a House which is nearly two-to-one Democratic, that it inevitably sends to the floor legislation that goes far beyond what other members of the House are willing to support.

The best and most important example in terms of long-range political significance came soon after I arrived in Washington. It was, in fact, a relatively minor bill with a name that sounded like a cross between a common cold and a sinus condition—the common situs bill—and despite a major controversy over the bill in labor and business circles a couple of years before, it came to the House floor virtually unnoticed by anybody else.

If the House passed it—as it had, overwhelmingly, two years before, and seemed almost certain to do again—a striking labor union which represented workers for a single contractor at a construction site would have been permitted to extend the strike to enlist unions in a walkout that could ultimately shut down the entire project. This "extended" strike, or "secondary" boycott, as it is called, is now illegal. If the common situs picketing bill had passed, such strikes would have been legalized in the construction industry.

Obviously, the legislation would have given labor unions a potent new bargaining and organizing tool, but at its worst the legislation would affect only one industry. It was certainly not the kind of sweeping across-the-board type of labor-management issue that would affect all employees and all workers (as a minimum wage increase would, for example). Had the bill passed it would have been of major philosophical importance, perhaps, but of only limited importance otherwise.

But it *did not* pass, and its defeat sent shock waves through the political community that are still being felt, signaling the beginning of a long, steady decline in labor-union influence in Washington.

It was without question an important political battle, and even more so for me. I had been a member of Congress for less than 90 days when the bill came to the House floor, and for the first time I played a role in a major political decision. It was heavy stuff.

Labor anticipated an easy victory. In fact, even we who were opposing the bill were anticipating an easy labor victory. During the 1976 elections the various labor union political action committees had been even more effective than usual, and large numbers of House members had been helped in part by sizable labor union contributions.

During that campaign my opponent had been quoted as saying: "If the unions support a man they know what he's going to do. They know who their friends are; when it comes to a vote, they're not going to be disappointed."

We did not expect them to be disappointed this time either. The last time the bill had come to the House floor, it had passed by a large margin; only a last-minute letter-writing campaign by national business organizations had persuaded then-President Gerald Ford to back away from earlier commitments and veto the bill.

Now organized labor was confidently getting ready to try again. About the time the bill was reported from committee, I was invited to a strategy meeting to plot the campaign to win the fight on the floor.

This was the smoke-filled political room. Only it wasn't filled with smoke, it was filled with paper. We met in the large corner office belonging to Ohio's John Ashbrook, who later became the top-ranking Republican on Education and Labor. (Ashbrook died suddenly, tragically, during the 1982 elections, while he was campaigning for a seat in the U.S. Senate. He was only 53.)

John Ashbrook was one of the most popular members of the House. He was a true believer with a quick mind, and his genial, friendly style—even when he was at his prickliest best—helped him pass an unusually large number of the amendments he offered.

But John Ashbrook, if he reminded us of anyone, reminded us all of our teen-age sons or daughters whose rooms have become so piled with "things" that one never knows for sure whether or not there's anything alive in there. Frank Thompson, who was one of Ashbrook's friends, even though they seldom agreed on anything more controversial than the date, called John "Trashbrook," or "Trash" for short. It's a term that in no way reflected on how anybody felt about John Ashbrook; it's just that one had to fight through such a stack of paper to find John's feet—or legs, for that matter. (Thompson, too, is gone from the House. "Thompy," as liberal as Ashbrook was conservative, was indicted in the Abscam scandal and defeated for re-election.)

Ashbrook was a newspaper publisher. Like most newsmen, he loved newsprint. If there is any man in public life who read more—more newspapers, more magazines, more bulletins—than John Ashbrook, he has yet to be discovered, and probably won't be until somebody comes through the House chamber with a bulldozer. John was, of course, invariably well-informed, and probably knew more about what was happening in his own congressional district than anybody else in Congress, but the price he paid was enormous: stacked papers on floors, chairs, laps, and in the aisles. If you sat down next to John on the House floor you'd probably find yourself sitting on a stack of newspapers from Johnstown, Newark, Mansfield, or some other small Ohio town.

Which should have warned me about what it would be like in John's office.

There were about half a dozen of us in the early meetings: Ashbrook, John Erlenborn (of Illinois), representatives of the National Association of Manufacturers, Associated Builders and Contractors, U.S. Chamber of Commerce and Associated General Contractors, and myself. We sat on sofas and chairs in one corner of Ashbrook's massive office (although he had a great deal of seniority he passed up moves to the fancier Rayburn Building to lay claim to one of the older, roomier corner offices in the ancient Longworth Building).

Stacks, reams, files, piles of papers—notes, briefings, legislative drafts, overflowed from the desk and tables to the floor. We huddled in a corner afraid of what might emerge from the stacks on the floor.

And in that room, primarily under the leadership of Ashbrook and the AGC's Warren Richardson, we began to discuss possible amendments, committee strategies, and the interminable head counts which funneled into that room in meeting after meeting, the results of hundreds of phone calls and personal visits constitutents had made to virtually every Member of the House. Slowly, as the business community let Congressmen know how much the vote meant to them, the gap narrowed. We began to fill long columns of names with plus marks and minuses, dividing up names of members who might be swayed.

And as the day for the vote neared, it was clear that we were still going to lose.

We went before the rules committee, which must assign a "rule" (a procedure for debate) before the bill could be considered on the floor. We rehashed our arguments against the bill, persuading nobody, urging, unsuccessfully, that a rule be denied, that the bill be killed on the spot.

Our strategy became desperately simple. We would try to come as close as possible to give ammunition to our counterparts in the Senate, led by freshman Senator Orrin Hatch, of Utah, who would then lead a filibuster (a weapon we don't have in the House) to try to block final passage when the bill got over there. We had precious little hope of actually defeating the bill in the House, where the first vote would occur.

As part of the strategy, we elected to offer as few amendments to the bill as possible. That, of course, is always a difficult decision. Faced with what you consider to be a bad piece of legislation, and the possibility that it will soon become law, the temptations are great to offer amendments that will at least make the bill better than it might be otherwise. But in this case we decided to play a different hand. The business community had mounted a powerful lobbying effort, and a number of Congressmen had indicated they might break away from labor to vote against the bill. Any "improvements" in the bill could give those swaying votes an option to stick with the committee and the labor contributors who had helped elect them, telling the business community that the bill just wasn't all that bad anymore.

It was a high-risk strategy, and one we knew could backfire, leaving us with an even worse bill than we might have had otherwise.

Near the end of the debate, the ranking Republican on the Committee, Al Quie, a quiet, thoughtful man who had won a reputation in the House for an unusually good share of common sense, offered an amendment to improve the bill. Had his amendment passed, Quie would have supported the bill, and that might well have assured its passage. But Thompson and Ford, certain of victory, refused the compromise and the amendment was defeated.

Then another Republican, Ron Sarasin, of Connecticut, offered a surprise substitute—a bill only slightly better than the original. If his substitute passed we were certain the ballgame would be all over.

And it *did* pass. Sarasin's substitute became the principal bill on the floor. The bill had been improved slightly—though, in our opinion, it was still seriously flawed—and our slender chances of victory were obviously lost. The next vote, on final passage, would be another vote on the same bill the House had just approved as a replacement for the original committee bill.

As the votes registered on the electronic tallyboard we stood with our eyes fixed on the changing totals. I stood at one door, cornering members as they came to the floor, arguing, persuading, pleading. Ashbrook and Erlenborn stood at other doors. Thompson and Ford stood with us, our thumbs down and their thumbs up. Out in the hallways, the clogged aisles leading into the House chamber, business and labor and White House lobbyists shouted to Congressmen as they rushed in for the vote, grabbing them, pleading with them, signaling them.

And then it was over.

We had won.

Ashbrook and I just looked at each other, our mouths open in amazement. What had happened? We didn't know. And it was clear from the stunned looks on their faces that Thompson and Ford didn't know either.

It had been a cinch, a sure, easy, early labor victory to set the pattern for the rest of the 95th Congress—and, in fact, it *did* set a pattern, though not in the way any of us had predicted, for after that labor won virtually nothing on the House floor, and has won virtually nothing since.

It was a special, almost eerie, occasion for me. In the excitement of the past week I had lost track of day and date. I looked down at the newspapers Ashbrook had left strewn on the floor. It was March 23rd. Patrick Henry's famous speech about liberty—"Give me liberty or give me death!"—had been delivered on March 23rd, and in celebration of that speech, which roughly summed up my own philosophy of government, I had announced my own candidacy for Congress in downtown Oklahoma City on another March 23rd—one year to the day before the common situs victory that has so completely changed the direction of labor-management politics in the Congress.

Many of the players in that battle are gone. Al Quie left the Congress at the end of that term and was elected governor of Minnesota, receiving much of the credit for carrying two Republican senators into office along with him. Ron Sarasin also ran for Governor, in Connecticut, but lost.

Warren Richardson, who had led the head-counting campaign for the Associated General Contractors, went into business for himself. He was later nominated for a high-ranking position in the Reagan Administration, but withdrew after coming under fire for having worked at one time for Liberty Lobby, a right-wing organization in Washington often accused or racism and anti-semitism.

And of course, Thompson is gone, and Ashbrook is dead.

It was a great victory and for the first time I felt myself a real part of the Congress, a man of some influence and even a small share of the power of Washington.

Later that week, still outfitting our newly leased home in the Virginia suburbs, my wife and I went shopping. We found part of what we wanted at Sears and attempted to pay by check. We needed identification, of course, and I proudly handed over my Congressional ID card. The clerk looked at it, handed it back, and asked if we had any other identification.

2. The Sinking of the Sequoia

When I came to the Congress, I asked my friends to judge me not by how much legislation I passed, but by how much I stopped.

I hope now that they're judging me by effort as well as success.

I do know that among other things, I've managed so far to sink one ship temporarily (which probably saved the taxpayers a million dollars), disrupt temporarily the building of a sumptuous new palace for the Imperial Senate, make a minor cut in a major program (I could have cut more if it hadn't rained), and save $2 million a year by not asking you what you think.

Early in May, 1978, the Interior Committee took up another of Phil Burton's unending string of minor park bills. This time Phil had outdone himself. We had before us a bill that looked as though it had been crafted to provide a new park for every member of the committee—and maybe even for every Member of the House. Instead of a pork barrel, it was a park barrel.

As I sat thumbing through the bill, which I had seen for the first time only minutes before, Bob Bauman leaned over to me holding a copy of the bill opened to a rather unique provision.

Sandwiched among parks and wilderness areas, Burton had placed a simple provision which had so far received no debate and no discussion. He wanted to buy a boat.

The *Sequoia* was a beached yacht, formerly a part of the White House fleet of yachts, limousines, airplanes and golf carts. Presidents had from time to time fished from it, played cards on it, sunbathed on it, boozed on it, lobbied businessmen and Congressmen on it, dined on it, entertained on it, and perhaps even made great decisions on it, though if that was the case those moments were not properly recorded. Richard Nixon had floated down the Potomac on it. Jimmy Carter had subsequently sold it, though whether or not it was because Nixon floated on it isn't certain.

The businessman who bought it paid $200,000 and tried to turn it into a tourist attraction. It did not prove to be much of an attraction.

So that owner sold it to another, a South Carolina businessman who was planning to drop anchor at Myrtle Beach and charge history buffs an admission fee to walk the decks—presumably thinking they were going to be putting their feet on the very same boards on which Lyndon Baines Johnson, for example, had put his feet (actually the yacht had been completely refurbished—new planks and all—since Johnson and his feet had been on board).

Apparently Burton, a sensitive man, was offended by the thought of people scuffing about in the Presidential footsteps without proper federal supervision, so this omnibus parks bill gave a new dimension to the word "omnibus" by tossing in an unlimited appropriation for the National Park Service to buy the yacht back and set it up as a proper exhibit in Washington.

From the information available to us, it looked like that open-ended appropriation might turn out to be as much as a million dollars. The federal government is not, of course, a profit-making venture, but even people who buy the Brooklyn Bridge could be expected to do better than that—a 400 percent loss in a single year.

I informed Burton, and the committee, that I planned to offer an amendment to strike the provision to buy back the boat. While I have a great love of history, that love has its limits, and somehow the *Sequoia* didn't seem to fit into those bounds—at least not at a cost of a million dollars.

In addition, I was more than a bit disturbed by the continuing tendency to create an "Imperial Presidency" in the United States, and felt there had to be a limit to the official adoration bestowed on our frequently unadorable presidents, a limit short of buying up every board upon which a presidential foot has trod, or every chair which has been warmed by a presidential posterior.

I said I would demand a recorded vote on my amendment. With an election six months away, not many members of Congress were likely to vote to spend a million bucks so their constituents would have something else to see if they ever got to Washington. It was a direct hit. The request for the appropriation was dropped and the *Sequoia* slipped beneath the waves.

3. A Palace for the Senate

Three months after the Interior Committee scuttled the *Sequoia*, I found myself again fighting against the somewhat expensive trappings of the imperial grandeur to which Washington was becoming accustomed.

On August 17, 1978, quiet, courtly old George Mahon, then the chairman of the Appropriations Committee, presented to the House a conference report on a bill providing supplemental appropriations to keep a number of federal agencies operating for the rest of the fiscal year.

After the original bill had passed the House, the Senate had added a small item: nearly $55 million to proceed with a new Senate Office Building—a marble palace with an original price tag, in 1972, of $48 million. Now, six years later, $16 million had already been spent and another $32 million appropriated—enough to pay for the building under the original cost estimates. But now there were new estimates—as much as $135 million—and the $55 million the Senate was seeking was only a stopgap partial payment on the remaining cost.

That the Senate could seriously propose such things in the midst of a great national debate over the extent of federal spending is probably a natural result of the principal difference between the House and Senate—the six-year term to which senators are elected. Thomas Jefferson recognized that fact when he wrote: "The purest republican feature in the government...is the House of Representatives. The Senate is equally so the first year, less the second, and so on." (Actually, it may work in reverse. A senator may be least responsive to public sentiment in his first year—when the next election is six years away—and most responsive in his sixth year—the year he runs for re-election.)

When the appropriations bill came before a conference committee to resolve differences between the House and Senate versions, the House conferees had quietly accepted the Senate request. Under the so-called rules of comity between the House and Senate (I'll scratch your back if you'll scratch mine.), the House doesn't question "internal" expenditures by the Senate, and the Senate doesn't question "internal" expenditures by the House. It's an unwritten "understanding" that is seldom violated.

Mahon clearly expected the entire House to go along, as it always had, and as the House conferees had. As he proceeded through the bill, I stood at a microphone, listening for the right moment in the reading to challenge the appropriation.

I was a freshman, a first-term member of Congress, just past my 41st birthday. Mahon had been in the Congress 43 years—longer than I had been alive. In a month he would be 78 years old. No member of Congress was more respected. A few months before, when he had taken to the floor to compliment me on a speech I had given, I had felt an unashamed pride. I reminded myself, however, that I was preparing to challenge not Mahon, but a massive new building that had been described by the *Washington Star,* as a new "Taj Mahal." Mahon, who was as much a part of the House tradition as he was a champion of it, had long been known for his fiscal conservatism and was, in this case, merely trying to uphold custom. Upholding custom, on the other hand, has never been my style.

The proposed building was opulent beyond most modern standards. The Senate already had two gymnasiums (one for each 50 Senators) and a swimming pool, but no tennis court at all, anywhere, so the new building was to include yet another gymnasium, this time with a tennis court. The Senate already had two restaurants for its members, but no rooftop restaurant, and so the new building was to include a rooftop restaurant. There was to be extra-thick marble, and the members of the Senate were to work in offices with wood-paneled walls running up to ceilings 16 feet high. Sacrifice, after all, should have its limits.

The Congress takes its traditions seriously, and I took Mahon seriously. Challenging either was not only bad form but unwise politics. And yet $55 million was at stake for a degree of legislative elegance I could not find much sympathy with.

The House completed action on the conference report as a whole and then, according to its procedure, moved to take up, one at a time, those provisions on which the House and Senate were technically in disagreement—those which had been in one version of the bill or the other, but not both, and to which one house or the other now had to "recede" from its position and "concur" with the language proposed by the other body.

When the reading clerk got to the item calling for the Senate office building appropriation, I took the floor:

"We are trying to match the palaces and coliseums of Rome," I said. "But the old Roman empire is gone—gone because it knew no restraints, because it had no will power, because it couldn't say 'no.'

"We have to learn to say 'no.'

"We are being asked to approve $55 million so legislators can become accustomed to sitting in richly appointed offices with wood paneling 16 feet high."

Among the House rules is one that specifically prohibits direct reference to the Senate (it is, in House discussion, "the other body") and criticism of the Senate by House members (or vice versa) simply is not done. As I spoke I could hear the buzz of other members on the floor as they whispered to each other.

"We have several legislative restaurants but no rooftop restaurant at all, so we are asked to take money from the pockets of our constituents to build a rooftop restaurant. We have gymnasiums—but no tennis courts, and so we are asked to take money from our constituents to build another gymnasium with a tennis court...

"These are not buildings that are being built. They are monuments to the ability of the Congress to thumb its nose at the people of this country."

Persons supporting the expenditure argued that the construction of the building had already been authorized and construction had already started; discontinuing construction at this point, they said, would leave an uncompleted and ugly shell, and waste the millions of dollars that had already been spent.

But those, as I pointed out, were not the only options. It was not too late to make some architectual modifications to change this project from a marble palace into an office building.

There is a good possibility, in fact, a likelihood, that if the House had taken up the issue on its own it never would have approved such an expenditure, at least not during an election year. The major argument against the striking of the appropriation now was the tradition of comity, each house turning a blind eye to the whims of the other.

"But we are not building this palace with our own funds; we are taking $135 million—*at least* $135 million—out of the pockets of the taxpayers—including the middle- and low-income taxpayer for whom we express such sympathy," I said.

"Some of the people who will pay for our edifice complex are my constituents. Some of that money is their money."

I had one other factor on my side. The debate was taking place on the last day the House was in session before the Labor Day recess. Within hours, members of Congress would be boarding airplanes to return to their congressional districts, and their votes on this issue would be fresh in the minds of the constituents who met with them at neighborhood meetings, coffees and civic club meetings.

"Today," I said, "you are going home to face your voters and I cannot imagine that you want to go home and face them having gone along with the building of a great marble monument to excessive government."

Mahon rose to answer me, basing his argument primarily on the long-standing tradition of harmony between the two houses. The Senate *had* looked away, after all, while the House built the Rayburn Building, *its* marble monument.

When Mahon had finished, Steve Symms took the floor. Steve is a lean, tall Idaho cowboy who wears cowboy boots and cowboy clothes, even though he grows apples, not cows. Steve Symms is a bold, boyish cowboy iconoclast, with an easygoing "aw-shucks" grin that sometimes allows him to take controversial positions without getting people angry (or, as cowboys say, without raising their hackles). This issue, though was a natural hackle-raiser, as we were to discover soon after Steve called for the vote.

As the clerk rang the bells to bring absent members to the floor, Symms and I headed for the doors with handbills. "Vote no. Don't go back and face your voters" (gentle persuasion) "after having approved $55 million to build a new marble palace for 100 Senators."

We won, 245-123.

In the real world, where decisions are sometimes final, the next step, obviously, would have been for the capitol architects to revise their plans and come back to the Congress with a *reduced* request. The Senate would still have its new office building, but one less in keeping with the imperial image, and the taxpayers would have retained at least a portion of the money that was to have come from their pockets. All in all, a happy ending.

As it turned out, that was more beginning than end.

The Senate chamber is only a short distance from the House floor, and within minutes after the vote a furious Robert Byrd, then the majority leader in the Senate, had phoned House leaders to find out who had blocked the building funds. Already Senate leaders were demanding guarantees from House leaders that the decision would be reversed. There were thinly veiled threats as well—pointed reminders that legislation approved in the House had to find its way through the Senate before it could become law.

The appropriation request did not come back to the House that year. Now that the issue had become public, and House members had gone on record in opposition to the expenditure, it would take a great deal of pressure, indeed, to force them to switch their votes while opponents back home scoured the daily newspapers looking for campaign issues.

When the Congress returned to work in 1979, however, with elections again two years distant, Senate leaders again began to dream of wood and marble and leisurely lunches overlooking lobbyists, staffers and taxpayers on crowded Constitution Avenue.

Within a year after the original vote, the House and Senate clashed again on a major appropriations bill, this time with dark hints in the background that Senators remembered clearly what the House had done to them on the "Taj Mahal" issue.

What was at stake was this: the House had already passed 12 major appropriations bills, but most of them were still in the Senate where they had not been acted upon. By mid-October of 1979, the Congress was in a bind because the government had run out of money to pay federal workers, including members of the armed services. Without the approval of the appropriations bills, most activities of government were going to have to be shut down; government employees were going to go without checks; veterans benefit checks would be held up; social security checks would be stopped; servicemen would not be paid.

In an attempt to get around the lack of action in the Senate, members of the House Appropriations Committee drafted a "continuing appropriation" bill that would continue funding at the same levels as previously until new legislation was passed. Both houses passed the continuing appropriation and sent it to a Conference Committee to resolve differences between the House and Senate versions of the bill.

But there were two major stumbling blocks. The first was a cost-of-living pay raise the House had included for members of Congress, including the Senate. The second was a serious conflict over whether or not federal taxpayers should pay for abortions for persons on welfare. The Senate bill authorized federally-funded abortions; the House version prohibited them.

I had voted against the pay raise, and so had the majority of the House, several times. But the House leadership had persisted and finally succeeded in winning approval of a 5.5 percent increase. The Senate had opposed the increase. Now, Senators, trying to pressure the House into backing down and accepting the Senate version of the bill, began to go before television cameras and newspaper reporters, where they virtually ignored the strong House sentiment on the abortion issue and sharply criticized House members, claiming that disagreement over the pay raise was the major stumbling block and chiding the House for tying up the whole federal government in order to get a piddling pay raise.

The Congress clearly did not deserve a pay increase; few members of either body—all making more than $57,000 a year—cared much about a $100 pay raise that was going to be difficult to justify and even more difficult to explain to angry voters. The pay raise was not the heart of the issue, abortion was. But the Senate could not resist the chance to get back at the House.

The Senate attacks infuriated House members, including those who had opposed the pay raise. At one bitter meeting of House and Senate conferees the new chairman of the House Appropriations Committee, Jamie Whitten, and the top-ranking Republican on the committee, caustic, sharp-tongued Silvio Conte, reminded Senators that the only reason the small pay raise was so insignificant to the Senators was that the Senate had quietly on unrecorded vote rescinded a previously adopted limitation on outside earnings, which the House continued to follow. As a result, although both houses are equal in rank and authority, and members of both houses are supposed to receive equal pay, House members were then restricted to receiving slightly more than $8,000 a year in outside earned income, including honorariums for speeches and articles, while Senators continued to earn many times as much—sometimes nearly tripling their official salaries.

Conte angrily pulled out an issue of *Congressional Quarterly* and jabbed his finger at Senators around the table who had been outspoken in criticism of the $100-a-month pay raise voted by the House. Pointing to Muskie, to Goldwater, to Magnuson, Conte pointed out that the most vocal critics of the raise had in fact themselves earned $100,000 or more in extra income during the previous year, something forbidden to House Members.

Needless to say, that exchange did not improve the deteriorating relationship between the two houses.

I had warned in the 1978 debate that if the appropriations request for the new building were brought back before the House, I would be waiting for it and would stop it again.

In fact, when it came back I didn't say a word.

There are at least three major aspects to every Congressman's job.

The first, and most obvious, is the continuing philosophical struggle to determine the size and power of the federal government, and the basic directions, social, political, and international, in which the country will move. This is a part of the job which concerns some Congressmen greatly, almost to the exclusion of other matters, and which concerns others not at all.

The second and most time-consuming—and the most important, politically—is the relationship between the Congressman and the people he represents. This includes not only constant communication with constituents in the form of meetings, newsletters, and replies to letters, but also the awesome task of trying to assist with the myriad difficulties that arise between citizens and the scores of federal agencies which either regulate them or dispense benefits (social security checks, veterans benefits) or welfare.

Finally, the Congressman serves as an extension of the various city and township governments in his district, and of the various chambers of commerce, in seeking to help the communities by bringing in industry and seeing to it that each community receives its proper share of the funds distributed under federal programs. (For a Congressman who favors great reductions in the size of government, this activity is defensible on the theory that even the member would not have voted for the program in the first place, now that it is in existence, and his constituents are helping to pay for it, they should get some of the benefits they are paying for rather than have their money spent elsewhere.)

In Oklahoma, as in much of the water-poor West, water is as price-less as gold. Man-made lakes and reservoirs are essential to community survival.

When I took office in 1977, two communities in my district were deeply involved in efforts to win federal approval and funding of water projects that had already been mapped out by the federal government.

McGee Creek Reservoir, in southeastern Oklahoma, was planned to provide water for eastern Oklahoma County, including the east side of Oklahoma City. Arcadia Lake, near the small city of Edmond, was being counted on to provide that city with 11 million additional gal-lons of water a year, without which the community's rapid growth would come to a halt.

A bill including funding for the McGee Creek and Arcadia proj-ects had been passed by the House but still had not been approved by the Senate when the renewed request for the office building appropria-tion came back to the House as part of a catch-all appropriations bill.

This time, with the two water projects still pending in the Senate, I kept quiet and let others fight—a classic example of the way expedi-ence sometimes takes precedence over principle.

In 1980, Steve Symms became a Senator himself. He now has an office in the Taj Mahal.

4. The Amendment that Failed the Night it Rained in Baltimore

Civics teachers may like to point to backroom bargaining and long lunches with lobbyists, but the fate of legislation often hangs on far flimsier threads.

For example, a controversial and expensive federal program, unani-mously recommended for extinction by one of the most powerful com-mittees in the Congress, once was saved because it rained in Baltimore.

Late in the first session of the 96th Congress, at the end of Septem-ber 1979, the House took up consideration of amendments to the Do-mestic Service Volunteer program—the so-called ACTION and VISTA programs, which use federal funds to train volunteers and fun-nel them into jobs within their communities.

Although there was never a serious attempt to do away with the programs themselves, a major controversy had developed over one portion of VISTA—a set-aside of 20 percent of the program's funds (more than $8 million) to pay for grants which in the past had sometimes gone to left-wing activist groups which had disrupted a national Democratic convention, organized lobbying efforts in state legislatures and passed out literature to volunteers picturing segments of the private sector as "the enemy."

This set-aside, the so-called "National Grants" program, had never been approved by the Congress. When the Domestic Service program was signed into law it contained provisions for grants to applicants selected either on a state or regional (multi-state) basis. Grants were to be awarded competitively, to non-profit organizations, to be used to provide volunteers to help out in low-income or "poverty" neighborhoods.

A strange thing happened, however. After the applications had been screened and the grants awarded, there was still money left over. Some $4 million, in fact. The demand was not as great as the Congress, in its generosity, had supposed.

This, of course, left two options: the agency could return the money to the treasury or spend it. The first option, in government, is unthinkable. But if it was unthinkable to return the money, it was impossible to spend it, because there were no more qualified applicants either on a state level or a multi-state level.

At that point, Sam Brown, the program's director, who had learned to improvise while organizing the national protests against the Vietnam war, improvised. He created, on his own, without congressional sanction, an additional grant program—he called them "National" grants—and began to divide up the remaining $4 million.

Soon the money was gone. And the program, which had been relatively free of controversy, began to be rocked by allegations of improper grants to ineligible recipients doing ill-advised things with their sudden wealth.

Criticism reached a crescendo, and the House Appropriations Committee ordered its non-partisan investigative staff to undertake a study of the program.

The investigators found that grants had been awarded on a noncompetitive basis, often to close friends and colleagues of the director, Sam Brown; that the volunteers were sometimes assigned to profitmaking organizations in violation of the law, and that the ultimate beneficiaries of the program often were not the poor, but middle-income activists.

For seven months, the investigators pored over the grant records, studied applications, interviewed state officials, and finally responded with a report (later approved unanimously by the committee) which suggested, among other things, that the Congress consider doing away with the National Grants program.

At that point, the scene shifted from the Appropriations Committee, which has authority over funding of the program, to the House Education and Labor Committee, which authorizes the programs and makes funding recommendations. The subcommittee on Select Education, which has original jurisdiction, took up a bill to continue the Domestic Service programs, and increase their funding, and passed the bill to the full committee with a favorable report after six days of hearings (compared to the seven-month investigation by the Appropriations Committee.

In the meantime, though, opposition to the programs had suffered a serious setback when overeager Republican staff members allowed their rhetoric to get ahead of their facts and persuaded Republican members of the subcommittee to make a series of unprovable allegations of misconduct and impropriety against the grant recipients. Although there were many justifiable criticisms and legal limits had sometimes been ignored or waived, the excessive accusations backfired. Embarrassed Republican members of the Subcommittee, caught out on a limb without documentation, were made to look foolish—a blow that was never quite overcome.

When the bill came to the full committee, I offered an amendment that would have stricken the funds for the National Grants program, leaving the funds included in that program to be allocated instead to qualified state and regional applicants on a competitive basis.

I had not been a member of the subcommittee which had considered the bill originally, and the same committee staff members who had advised using a heavy hand in those hearings now attempted to steer me in the same direction. I've been caught off base before, like most people who sometimes have to rely on others for briefings and information, and I've developed a great sense of caution about making allegations of any kind. I not only insist on seeing the documentation myself (It's not enough to be told we have it), I approach the issue as though I were arguing the other side. Like most people I have no desire to be embarrassed, especially in public, and don't want to be caught making statements I can't prove (or, worse, that can be disproved or punched full of holes).

What's more, as my own staff members have learned, heavy rhetoric—rightwing, leftwing, or any other kind—leaves me cold.

So I insisted on doing it my way. I focused on the unauthorized nature of the national grants, the spending of money that could have been saved, the waiving of important criteria, the lack of competitive bidding for the money.

At this point, of course, having stood firm on principle, I should have won. I didn't. It did make me feel better, but I didn't change the outcome at all. We knew before the amendment was offered that it would be defeated on a straight-party-line vote, Republicans for it, Democrats against it (the usual procedure in that committee), and that is exactly what happened. Nonetheless, at that point we had an amendment we could talk about in the committee report and take to the House floor where we would have a better chance of success.

All in all, a lot of work and strategy preparing for a showdown that ultimately would be decided on the basis of a fight over abortion, a congressional pay raise and a baseball game that wasn't played.

I proceed from this point with an apology to every teacher who ever drew boxes and lines on a blackboard to illustrate "how a bill becomes a law." If they had only known!

On September 29, a Friday, weeks after the committee had completed action on the bill, the House was in a typical Friday session, preparing to adjourn not only for the weekend, but this time for a week off in commemoration of Columbus Day, that being as good an excuse as any to let House members go back to their districts to be seen.

As a rule, Friday sessions (when there are any) end at 3 p.m. so Congressmen can flood the local airports for the early evening flights out of Washington. As usual, many had left early—Thursday night or early Friday—knowing they would not be likely to miss many votes.

This Friday, however, was not as typical as it seemed. The House and Senate had by then passed their different versions of that "continuing appropriation" to provide money to pay Social Security recipients, servicemen, judges, Congressmen and other important people—the same bill that was to lead to such bitterness between the two houses. (This "unusual" step, a continuing appropriation, is necessary in every session because the Congress, for one reason or another, never gets around to passing its appropriations bills on time.)

The principal differences in the two versions, as I've explained, were a dispute over a congressional pay raise and two different views about the use of federal funds to pay for abortions. Because nothing could happen until both houses agreed on the same bill, representatives of both chambers (conferees) were locked in a struggle in a joint committee meeting (a conference committee), where each house would seek concessions and make them until the two bills came into sync.

On this day, each House seemed able only to snarl in contempt at the intransigence of the other. The day dragged on without agreement. (In fact, it was at about this time that Jamie Whitten and Sil Conte were building to the blow-up point over the Senate's criticism of the pay raise provision.)

The complication was this: As soon as the House finished its business, having elected to go on recess, it would be gone—scattered to the hills, dales and metroplexes—and could do nothing more until it reassembled, a week after the money ran out. It became necessary somehow to keep the House in session while the conferees debated and fought.

From noon on, on this day when nothing much was supposed to happen, there were a dozen recorded votes as one bill after another was brought up without notice to fill the gap. Three o'clock became four and five and six and seven.

And in this atmosphere, the House leadership suddenly called up the Domestic Service amendments, on a day when this wasn't expected, with two key players—the ranking Republican member of the committee, John Ashbrook, of Ohio, and the ranking Republican member of the subcommittee, Colorado's Ken Kramer, already gone.

We attempted to stop consideration. I demanded a vote on approval of the rule to bring the bill up, and another on whether or not the House could "go into committee" (resolve itself into a fictitious "committee" in which it considers amendments). On each vote, as the day dragged on and members left to catch their flights, the number of votes grew smaller. If a quorum disappeared—and it almost did—the House would have had to either adjourn, giving everybody time to prepare adequately for the debate, or lock up the remaining members and order the others arrested and brought back to Washington. That, too, has been done.

Because nobody on either side was ready, we agreed that there would be two hours of debate, not just one as provided in the rules (though nobody had two hours' worth of things to say) and we would proceed to use up the first hour that day. That way we killed time and remained in session, but made sure there would be no votes on amendments that day since the amending process can't start until the general debate is finished.

That having been decided, it then became necessary to decide what to say. None of us on the floor had materials or speeches with us, having been caught completely by surprise. John Erlenborn of Illinois, the second-ranking Republican on the committee, after Ashbrook, took over floor management of our half of the debate, and while we scribbled notes from memory (the bill had been before the committee weeks before, and dozens of bills had been considered since) Marty LaVor, a committee staff member, rushed to the House floor and rummaged through his papers, providing typed speeches that had been prepared for somebody else to give. We made changes, filled in our own material, and used Marty's speeches. Across the center aisle, the bill's manager, subcommittee chairman Paul Simon, put together his side of the makeshift debate (presumably in much the same way, since he had only a few minutes more notice than we). Sometimes the politician's proverbial ability to talk at the drop of a hat is a necessary talent.

As all this was taking place, I had to miss my own flight back to Oklahoma City, where two friends, Gary Johnston and Earl Austin, were getting ready to throw a grand party at Gary's house—a fund-raising party for my next campaign. I missed it, as I had missed one the year before for a similar reason. Fortunately, I managed to get word to Gary in time for him to cancel the party. We had barely started, and already the debate had cost me several thousand dollars.

The House and Senate conferees never did get together that night. They split again and again over abortion, and when the matter came back to the House floor and we insisted on keeping our previous position, the Senators huffed and pouted and announced that all the agreements they had already reached on other points were out the window. So the House closed up shop and went on its recess, having resolved nothing, but at great expense to the voting attendance records of some 200 members of Congress who had headed home in the expectation that Friday, like others, would be a rather slow day.

On Tuesday, October 9, the day the House met again after the recess, we were ready, and the Domestic Services bill was brought up early in the afternoon. I had my amendment, my speech, hundreds of copies of a flyer which summarized what I was trying to do and which I had prepared to hand out at the doors to the House chamber as members came in to vote.

First came that important second hour of debate. Nobody wanted it. Kramer and Ashbrook each made opening statements, Ashbrook yielding most of his time, and after a few more general comments the debate was closed. The first amendment was brought up quickly and disposed of quickly. I was next up.

At that point, back came the House leadership with word that more action needed to be taken on those conference reports on the continuing appropriations. Again, we left the Domestic Services bill behind and went on to other things.

It was then 4 p.m. The only word we had received about a probable quitting time for the day was 5:30 "or later." I tried to pin down the Majority Leader, Jim Wright. Would we get back to the Domestic Services debate that day? He didn't think so. I checked with the Republican floor staff, which checked with the Democratic leadership, and also determined we would not get back to the bill that day. I asked Paul Simon; he didn't think so either.

This presented a rare opportunity. I had sent a letter to every member of Congress (co-signed by the Republican whip, Bob Michel), outlining my amendment and quoting from the Appropriations Committee report suggesting elimination of the National Grants program. But because of the Columbus Day recess nearly two weeks had passed since the letter had been received and we needed to refresh memories (we couldn't expect floor debate to do that since so few members listen to the arguments).

Dottie Strunk, my staff assistant and an expert on labor law, joined me on the House floor. We began to work on a floor strategy. We had never been overly optimistic—we were hoping only for a strong enough showing to force Sam Brown to back off on his controversial grants to political activists—but now we saw a chance for a concerted effort overnight that might make it possible to win on the floor.

I had strengthened my planned floor statement by getting (surreptitiously) a copy of the complete Appropriations Committee report, which had been mysteriously "unavailable" to us before. Now we saw a possibility of drafting a new and much more powerful letter. Because the bill would probably be brought up again the next day, we would have to hand-deliver the letters to every Congressional office overnight rather than sending them through the mail.

I felt then (and later, after seeing how many votes we had) that this one extra night could have offset the disadvantage of the ten-day recess and given us a good chance for victory.

But even as Dottie and I began to put together the strategy and draft a new letter, word began to circulate that the bill was coming back.

Paul Simon had been told to stay put. He didn't know, but thought it was a possibility we'd get back to the bill before the night was out.

"When will they decide?" I asked.

"Is it raining out?" he asked.

It had been a dark and threatening day. There had been intermittent drizzles, and heavier rains seemed imminent.

The schedule, it turned out, depended on the weather. House leaders were eager to close up shop and head for Baltimore, an hour away on the turnpike, to watch the Orioles and the Pittsburgh Pirates in the World Series. As soon as the appropriations debates were out of the way, we'd clear out, some back to our offices (to distribute letters) and others, presumably, to the stadium in Baltimore. If the game was rained out, of course, we'd stay in session.

At last, we finished work on the Appropriations bill. Paul Simon again took the floor. I looked outside. It was raining.

It had been two weeks since the members had received information about the amendment, although a few had watched the debate on television as they sat in their offices. Many were frank in admitting they had no idea what they were voting on, which is often the case. In such circumstances, most Republicans will follow the advice of the Republican at the door and most Democrats will follow their own leadership.

As it turned out, we stayed close until near the end, and ended up losing by a vote of 209-177, a much stronger showing than we had expected. It was enough to send a message to VISTA, and possibly to give us additional leverage if the Senate also took a slap at the National Grants program.

And it had another dividend. Under the previous law, Sam Brown had as much as 20 percent of the total Domestic Services budget available for discretionary grants. As a result of the opposition to the National Grants, the committee had cut the figure down to 18 percent, and now Simon told me he would agree to cut it still more, to 15 percent—a reduction of one-fourth in Brown's discretionary funds. Under the previous authorizations, there were simply not enough applications and thus there was a surplus that Brown then distributed through his new grant program. Assuming there would be a similar number of applications in the future, the reduction in Brown's discretionary authority could save the taxpayers as much as $2 million, not a bad outcome for a fight we didn't win.

5. How We Saved $2 Million by Not Asking You What You Think

One frequent criticism of the Congress is its apparent lack of concern for what the people think. "Are you going up there to vote the way *you* want to," we are asked, "or to represent us?"

The truth is, most members of Congress are somewhere between these two schools of thought.

Like most other members of Congress, I spend a considerable amount of time (and some of the taxpayer's money) trying to ascertain just how the people themselves feel about the issues that so clearly affect them.

In addition to the many opportunities we have to talk during my trips back to Oklahoma, I use questionnaires.

There are two kinds of questionnaires. The first, designed to assist me in my political campaigns, is conducted by a private polling firm once or twice a year, and is paid for with campaign funds, contributed voluntarily. Although no taxpayer has to pay for such polling, the results give me a detailed understanding of how the people in my district feel on a number of issues.

The second kind of survey, conducted several times a year through my newsletter to constituents, is paid for by the taxpayers, and goes to each home in the district (whereas the political survey goes to a scientifically-selected cross-section of voters).

These surveys tap public opinion on almost the entire range of issues scheduled to come before the Congress in a calendar year: energy, defense, economic issues, alternative programs for reducing inflation. One newsletter devoted an entire page to a lengthy summary of the federal budget, and asked constituents which items they felt should get more funds, which less, and which were being supported at about the right level.

All in all, it is a fairly extensive—if unprofessional—attempt to determine the principal concerns and philosophical leanings of the people I represent. Similar surveys are conducted by other Congressmen.

Then, Lou Harris, who takes polls for a living, and an Arkansas Congressman, Bill Alexander, a member of the House Democratic leadership, came up with an idea to do things a little better.

I first learned of the better idea when Guy Vander Jagt, the chairman of the Republican Congressional Committee, came to me on the House floor. John Rhodes had asked Vander Jagt to look into it. Vander Jagt asked me to do it.

As Speaker, Tip O'Neill had asked Alexander to put together a survey for the entire House. I was to represent Rhodes and the Republican leadership in the planning meetings.

The original concept was vague and highly generalized. Because polling by individual House members was uneven, both in quality and frequency, and there was no coordination between Congressmen as to the questions asked, Harris and Alexander were proposing professional surveys in 40 congressional districts, equally divided between districts represented by Republicans and districts represented by Democrats. No district would be polled without the consent of its representative. The results would be made public and distributed to the leadership of both parties and to all members.

Then, if the House seemed satisfied with the program, additional districts would be polled, at intervals, until eventually, in a year's time, the surveys would cover the entire nation.

As discussions began all this was no more than an idea—there was no discussion of structure, cost, contractual arrangements. Gradually, however, details—disturbing details—began to come into focus.

For one thing, Alexander and Harris seemed determined to inject a political conclusion into the polling from the start.

On September 28, 1980, Harris submitted an outline of his program. "The use of such a polling capability," the plan said, "would serve many important purposes:"

The first purpose described was this:

"1) We are living at a time in our history where the legislative process is singularly marked by effective use of the lobbying process by single-issue causes. These advocates are dedicated to one issue alone and are usually highly vocal or well-organized. Poll results such as these can put into proper context just how representative these single-issue causes are and how much they merely represent a vocal, albeit well-organized minority."

In an early meeting I expressed reservations about including such a statement in stating the underlying premise behind the polling since it contradicted the very objectivity that would be necessary for such a survey to be useful.

Was it necessarily wrong for members of Congress to give weight to the concerns of people whose principal political interests centered around a single issue or a single set of issues? Who was included? Right-to-life groups which opposed abortion? How about supporters of the Equal Rights Amendment? What about opponents of the Equal Rights Amendment? What about sportsmen who had focused most of their political activity on attempting to block any federal restrictions on gun ownership? What about labor unions? The medical profession? Oil companies? Groups like the Sierra Club, which were concerned almost exclusively with protecting the environment? One candidate for president, John Anderson, later announced publicly that he could not support any candidate for president who did not support the SALT treaty. Were all of these highly-focused concerns, and the rights of such concerned citizens to try to influence their representatives, to be muted by a blanket survey which gave equal weight to people who felt keenly on an issue and those who simply hadn't thought much about it yet?

In October, I showed up at the office of Frank Thompson of New Jersey, then the chairman of the House Administration Committee, to discuss a method for getting the proposal before Thompson's committee, which would have to recommend its approval to the entire House before any action could be taken. I invited Bob Badham, a Republican member of the committee, to attend the meeting with me, and while we waited for Alexander and Thompson to show up, I briefed him about the plan and explained some of the concerns which had begun to nag at me—the cost (still unrevealed); the whole idea of using taxpayers' dollars to conduct a survey which would certainly be used to help keep Congressmen in office (or by the political parties, to try to arm challengers running against incumbents). Badham shared my concern and expressed his own serious reservations about Republican participation in the plan.

Nearly 30 minutes passed; Thompson and Alexander didn't appear. Before I left, however, I instructed Henry Woods, Alexander's legislative assistant, to remove the "single-issue" comments from the draft.

When it came back to me, the revised resolution began this way:

"Whereas single-issue organizations continue to proliferate nationwide for the purpose of exerting extraordinary influence on the legislative process..."

Other parts of the package concerned me as well. For one thing, it was apparently preordained that Harris would receive the contract—and the attendant national publicity as the official pollster for the Congress—without the House seeking other bids. The September 28 proposal put it very simply: "The national firm of Louis Harris and Associates has agreed to provide the House with the needed professional capability to do this task."

I was concerned also about the tendency such a national survey would have to overshadow the results individual members received from questionnaires sent to people in their districts. While it is true that we are a national Congress, and that our acts affect the entire nation, it is not true that we act on the basis of a national sentiment. We do have a representative role to fill, even though we must each decide how much weight to give that role in our decision-making. I care how the people in my congressional district feel about a wide range of issues; I frankly am not as concerned with whether or not somebody in Frankfort, Kentucky, or Reno, Nevada, feels the same way. We each represent a single constituency, and it is from the pool of all those varied interests that we achieve a national consensus. For me to give equal weight to views from Oklahoma City and New York City would be to eliminate the representative function from a Congressman's job description.

I was determined not to let the Republican Party, or Rhodes, be manuevered into support for a program we could not defend in good conscience. Finally, in a meeting in my office, in December, I asked Harris for a full accounting of what such a program would cost. At first his answers were vague, but as bits of information were dropped I jotted the figures down on a note pad.

The totals were staggering:

The House was to supply Harris with 100 telephoners for each of nine seven-hour shifts. Their salaries were to be paid for by the taxpayers.

The House was to turn over to Harris more than 5,000 square feet of space, the space to be paid for by taxpayers.

The House was to provide, and the taxpayers were to pay for, 100 sound-proofed interviewing booths; 134 chairs; 17 desks; a file cabinet; a locked supply cabinet; a typewriter, with stand; a telecopier; a dry copier; 19 waste baskets; four pencil sharpeners; 60 feet of coat racks; coffee and soda vending machines; 10 shelving units; 100 telephones with individual WATS lines; six more phones with 20 buttons each; seven more phones with 10 buttons each, and, later, additional storage and filing equipment, construction of separate offices for Lou Harris employees, and a conference room.

The House would also provide all duplicating facilities and all computer facilities.

In addition to the prestige (and possible new business opportunities) that would naturally flow from its selection by the Congress, the Harris firm would have been paid $1,522,500 to conduct the surveys, plus another $522,000 to analyze the results—a total of more than $2 million.

The cost to the taxpayers would have been $2 million plus the cost of the phones, workers, chairs, desks, wastebaskets, computers, and so forth.

Alexander was eager to move forward with the proposal and wanted to rush it to the House floor as quickly as possible. I expressed my reservations and said I could not support the plan unless it was approved first by the entire Republican conference—the official caucus of all House Republicans.

I had concluded that the plan simply could not be justified, and reported back to Vander Jagt and Rhodes, expressing grave concerns about the idea. Then, to be certain it would not go further, I cornered influential Republicans on the House floor and described the plan to them. When they reacted strongly against the idea, as I knew they would, I reported their reactions back to Rhodes. Then I talked to other members who, I knew, had close ties to Washington political reporters. Within 24 hours a House doorkeeper told me that Mary Russell, a reporter for the *Washington Post*, was waiting outside to talk to me.

The story was in the *Post* on December 17. The better idea has not been heard from since.

6. Decision Making in Washington: A Rule of Thumb

Observing the Congress from the outside had somehow given me the impression that nobody in the place seemed to know what he (or she) was doing.

Fortunately, members of Congress are not always as uninformed as they seem. In fact, there are *several* ways House members make sure they cast their votes intelligently.

First, there is the rule of thumb. Every member who approaches the House chamber for a vote is confronted by a sea of tempting, pleading and threatening thumbs—some turned up, others turned down. The secret is to associate thumbs with (a) faces and (b) affiliations. For example, the thumbs may belong to (a) White House lobbyists; (b) labor lobbyists; (c) business lobbyists; (d) Democratic Party leaders; (e) Republican Party leaders; (f) sponsors of the bill; (g) sponsors of an amendment to change the bill, and so forth, advocates for everything from avocados to the Big Apple.

Here's how the system works:

A Republican Congressman walks up the Capitol steps and into lobby leading to the House chamber. If the President at the time is a Republican and the House is controlled by the Democrats, he usually supports the President and opposes the Democratic leadership. On the other hand, this is a vote that means a lot to organized labor, and there is a large, active labor union membership back home. He steps into the sea of thumbs, and this is what he finds:

(a) Up
(b) Down
(c) Up
(d) Down
(e) Up
(f) Down
(g) Up

How does he vote? Unfortunately, there are no thumbs that can make the final decisions on that. It would help immensely if thumb (b) would flip or thumb (a) would flop, but thumbs don't have a mind of their own. But, in any case, he now knows the political dimensions of the vote. For some members, that's enough.

In the early days of the Carter Administration, this system was somewhat of a problem because the people who came over from the White House didn't know who anybody was and didn't seem to care much. Some Congressmen, I suppose, eventually made their mark and even the Carter White House was able to figure out who they were; I know I didn't, because halfway through 1979 a Carter campaign aide in the White House called to ask me to work for the President's re-election.

The rule of thumb, however, is not the only scientific method used by House Members to make sure they know what they're doing.

There is also the reading test.

Above the House chamber, an electronic tote-board lights up at each recorded vote. Each member's name is on the board, with small lights beside each name. A red light indicates a "no" vote; a green light means "yes"; a yellow light means a member voted "present."

The reading test works this way. Congressman A charges into the House chamber in a state of confusion. At the door he asks "what are we voting on" (a frequent question on the House floor) but finds 30 other members asking the same thing. (He has to hurry; every member only has 15 minutes to vote, and sometimes it takes 14 of those minutes to get to the House floor.) Continuing to walk toward the front of the chamber, he keeps his eye glued to the board.

There's Congressman B—a fellow liberal/conservative/tobacco farmer/something or other (political kinship has many forms). A green light. A yes. How about Congressman C? If he voted "no," you know your vote is a "yes." He voted "no." In goes the card: a yes vote.

Just in time. Time runs out; the vote is over. Congressman A sits down beside B: "What was that last vote?" he asks.

There is, of course, another aspect to the reading test, especially for Congressmen from smaller states. It's seldom desirable to be out on a limb having to explain back home why your vote was different from everybody else's. So after checking philosophical bed-partners, board-leaders usually check other members of the state delegation, either on the board or at computer terminals which offer a quick read-out of the votes cast by every Republican, every Democrat, every member from Connecticut.

There is another method.

Perhaps the issue involves banking. You know little enough about banking and had trouble figuring out the interest on the loan you took out to get through the campaign, so you simply scan the rows looking for a member of similar persuasion who sits on the Banking Committee. "What is it?" you ask. "How should I vote?" and, later, after the voting is over, "why?"

And, finally, there is still another method, sometimes used. You simply carry a briefing paper, prepared by a legislative assistant. The paper states the bill's general provisions and arguments for (and against) it, including a summary of the mail or phone calls received from the folks back home. The member only has to read the paper, find the number of the bill before the House, match it to the number on the briefing sheet, and vote. This method has the disadvantage of leaving your legislative assistants with no time to do anything else, including work on your own legislative initiatives.

This is not to suggest that no members come to the floor with some understanding of what we're voting on, but quite often a member's philosophical consistency rests on how well he or she can navigate the thumbs and pass the reading test en route to the casting of a vote that must be accomplished in the next minute and forty-two seconds.

It is clear that while hearing ability and mental capacity are not always needed in the Congress, a good pair of eyes is an absolute must.

Part Two
A POLITICS OF VALUES

CHAPTER FOUR
CARING FOR THE PEOPLE:
A POLITICS OF SENSITIVITY

1. Paying for Results: How Much Is a Congressman Worth?

As inflation increases, and the congressional workload gets heavier, there is an increasing pressure to pay the Congress what it's worth.

Which is precisely what many Congressmen are afraid of.

Members of Congress currently receive $69,800 a year in official salary, although a good many are personally wealthy and have sources of outside income that increase their annual earnings to several times that much. There is a constant underlying pressure, however, to increase the salaries still more.

During my first term in Congress nothing else the House considered—not the labor issues, not the Humphrey-Hawkins bill, not even the Panama Canal treaties—brought as great a flood of mail, phone calls and telegrams as the Congressional pay raise.

I had opposed the pay raise—I suggested that we *reduce* congressional salaries by one percent every time inflation went up one percent—but it made no difference; we were *all* in hot water, whether for the raise or against it, and I was swamped with more mail than we could keep up with.

One radio station in my district dominates central Oklahoma in the evening, and stretches into 14 other states as well. That station (KTOK), has a nighttime call-in talk show which was then hosted by John Dayle, a gruff, bearded bear of a man who gives no quarter in his relentless hostility to the absurdities of big government. One night Dayle decided, on the spur of the moment, to send a telegram to all the members of the Oklahoma congressional delegation demanding that we vote against a congressional pay raise. He asked his listeners to

mail in their names (and a quarter, to help pay for the cost of the telegram); he promised to see that we got the message.

We got the message.

Within days I received a telegram from more than 7,000 of the station's listeners.

Why did so many Americans feel so strongly about the increase?
Congressional salaries had been increased in the past with far less notice. In fact, congressional pay had been ridiculously low until just a
dozen years before, and then had increased rapidly.

Is the pay level so far beyond reason as to be inherently objection-
able?

Though I have been constantly critical of the Congress and the
way it operates, there is no question that almost all members of
Congress—including, surprisingly, those who disagree with me—work
as hard as members of any other profession, and harder than most.
There is seldom a day off, and precious little time away from work on
workdays. The average congressional day lasts well into the evening,
and trips back to the congressional district to meet with constituents,
give speeches and hold town meetings take up most weekends and last
into the night-time hours. In Washington, there are frequently two,
and even three, committee meetings at the same time, and on days
when roll call votes are frequent it is not uncommon to see members of
Congress, including some well along in years, racing full-stride for the
equivalent of two or three blocks across the streets or through the underground tunnels of the Capitol in order to make it to the House floor
in time.

If one got paid for effort alone, few professions would have a right
to get paid more.

And its perhaps a bit awkward to suggest that Congressmen, the
men and women in charge of running the most powerful nation on
earth, are overpaid at $69,000 a year when rock singers, people who
write pornography, people who ride horses around racetracks and corporate executives who run Chrysler into near-bankruptcy earn several
times as much.

But there are other issues as well that make a debate over congressional salary legitimate.

For one thing, congressional pay comes out of your pocket. The
government takes the money away from you and there is precious little
you can do about it. If the Grateful Dead, Pete Maravich and Lee
Iacocca make $60,000 or $600,000 or $6 million a year, it's really little

of your concern or mine. If you don't want to cough up, you can simply skip their concerts, their ballgames, or their cars, and let somebody else pay if that's what he feels like doing.

Because every last penny of that congressional salary—before pay raise and after—comes out of your pocket, and because so much else seems to be coming out of your pocket these days, largely because of the Congress, you have a sound reason for being miffed when we want to take more.

Perhaps this will put the claim for higher congressional salaries into perspective.

1. Prices go up all the time, as we know, but *that's* not inflation; that's only a symptom of inflation, in the same way that rain causes wet streets and the wet streets are only a symptom, a sign that it's been raining. Inflation means a devaluation of the dollar; each dollar becomes worth less in terms of what it buys.

2. How does each dollar lose its value? If there is less demand for it, for some reason, it will become worth less, but the more common way is for each dollar to become worth less because there are more of them to cover the same amount of total value. When the government prints more money to cover the same amount of value (the gross national product), each individual dollar printed is worth less.

3. So why is more money printed if that's the case? Because the Congress has spent more. If Congress spends more money than it takes in (deficit spending), there are three principal ways in which it can make up the difference. It can (a) raise taxes. But politicians who raise taxes too much become former politicians. Or it can (b) go into the marketplace and borrow money from private lenders. It's already done so much of that that private businesses which need to borrow money to modernize equipment or expand (and thus create more jobs) can't do it; the government has soaked up the money. The third way (c) is to simply print it. Whether there's more value to back it up or not, if we need money to pay bills, then just print some. Sort of the way a counterfeiter does it, or the way you or I might if we owned a printing press in the basement and a good set of plates.

For years you had been unable to keep up with the cost of living, to set aside money in savings, to meet your mortgage payments, to plan on retirement—because inflation had gotten out of hand (your money was worth less and didn't buy as much), and inflation had gotten out of hand because the Dr. Spock generation of Congressmen, pampered beyond the ability to accept limits or restraints, kept spending more and more of your money (they went past the half-trillion-dollar-a-year mark sometime in 1978, and reached a trillion dollar national debt by 1981).

Which brings us back to the question of a pay raise.

Imagine that you are an employer and an employee asks you for a raise. That employee has been working hard, but persists in doing things wrong and as a result is hurting your business. Would he get the raise? You would undoubtedly decide that workers get pay raises for doing a good job and not just for showing up at work.

Then how can members of Congress ask for a raise?

Perhaps even in the case I've just described a point can be legitimately made that an employee who somehow has managed not to be fired should get at least a cost-of-living raise. After all, union contracts and even civil service work contracts provide for cost-of-living adjustments in exchange for merely showing up at work for a certain period of time and not getting fired. Students are routinely passed on to the next grade in school just for showing up. It's become a part of the system, the new American way, somewhat like a child getting an allowance just for breathing.

There are at least two important differences, however, when it's a Congressman who would be getting a raise. For one thing, when a Congressman's cost of living increases—and yours does—it's primarily because the Congress has *caused* the cost of living to go up. For a Congressman to get a raise under those circumstances is like the definition of *chutzpah:* the fellow who murders both parents and then throws himself on the mercy of the court because he's an orphan.

And for another thing, the pay raise the Congress voted for itself in 1977 was somewhat higher than the increase in the cost of living—and somewhat higher than your usual run-of-the-mill wage adjustment.

Granted, Congressmen have living expenses most folks don't have—the need for a second place to live (a home either in the Washington area or the Congressman's home district and usually an apartment, at least, in the other place), second sets of furniture, dishes, toiletries, utility bills, telephones, and so forth. Thus a $69,000 salary in the Congress is hardly comparable to the same amount of money somebody else might earn who is required only to have one home and one set of everything that goes in that home.

Nonetheless, when the Congress appropriates money to give itself a raise, even if it's either deserved or needed, it must—because it is taking that money from the pockets of the taxpayers—keep in mind not only the Congressman's need for the money but also the taxpayer's ability to pay it.

In 1977, the Congress gave itself a pay increase of about $13,000 a year—an increase that was more than most American families make in a year. The median income in my congressional district that year was $7,569, not much more than half what the Congress voted itself in additional pay on top of a salary that was already nearly $50,000 a year. Only 12 percent of the families in my district had family incomes above $15,000—and yet the Congress had voted itself nearly that much in extra pay, on top of a previous salary more than three times that $15,000 family income. (In fact, the pay raise was *so* much that it alone was almost as much as the median income in the Washington suburbs—Fairfax County, Virginia, and Montgomery County, Maryland—the two wealthiest counties in the country, where the federal bureaucrats live.)

The Congress was in the position of making it harder for the public to afford to pay what the Congressmen were already getting, and then taking a sizable increase to boot, all out of the same nearly-empty pockets.

Few issues, however, have been so hotly debated on the House floor, nor have many other issues—no matter how great their importance to the nation's future—stirred the same degree of animosity among House members. Even House Speaker Tip O'Neill and Majority Leader Jim Wright took the floor of the House to plead for the pay raise as younger members angrily denounced the gall of the Congress that would ask for more pay while it was urging citizens to tighten their belts. Privately, in the aisles and the cloakrooms, and behind the railing at the rear of the House chamber, younger members, or members with a record of narrow victory margins, urged their colleagues to vote for the increase. "I can't," they would say, "but I hope you can."

I personally believe I deserved a pay increase. I had devoted the two previous years of my life to trying to stop the federal government from spending so much of the taxpayer's money. But the issue was whether the Congress as a whole—all of us—had done such a good job that we deserved to be paid more.

It would be fair, I think, to look at the Congress in the same way any employer would look at an employee to determine whether or not a pay raise could be justified.

Between 1964 and 1980, federal spending had increased from approximately $100 billion a year to more than $600 billion a year, and as a result, the rate of inflation had increased from 0.5 percent a year in 1955 to 12.4 percent by the end of 1980, and federal taxpayers had so little money left in their pockets that the percentage of their incomes they were able to set aside in savings accounts dropped to 4.5 percent by 1980—the lowest savings rate since 1949.

Taxes were up so much that by mid-1980 it became obvious that soon the federal government was going to be taking in income and social welfare taxes a higher percentage of the gross national product than ever before in the nation's history—a higher percentage even than in 1944, the previous high, when the United States was fighting the Nazis and the Japanese.

And one area in which the Congress was clearly responsible for positive and farsighted action, providing for the national defense, had seen a rapid reduction in American military capability, reflected in a clearcut Soviet military superiority in missiles, tanks, ships, manpower, modern intercontinental and intermediate-range bombers—in fact, almost the entire panoply of a nation's armed strength.

The government, under the direction, oversight and financing of the Congress, had taken on more and more responsibility for protecting us.

However, in any business or activity, it's not promise that counts, but performance.

Sometimes, that point is made with the simple statement: Talk is cheap. But, of course it's not *always* cheap. Not when you're dealing with the government.

Those who advocate bigger and bigger government, who don't trust the private sector and think it is up to the government to keep us safe, have now succeeded in placing most of the responsibility for our health and safety in the hands of the federal government. Federal bureaucrats regulate everything from the speed limits on our highways to seatbelts on airplanes. And all that protection is costing us a lot of money.

Maybe the government *ought* to be in charge of these things *if* we can assume that we're all better off with Big Brother watching over us and tucking us in at night.

But, are we?

It's performance that counts, and the government is doing a pretty awful job. There is an assumption that the government can keep us safe better than the private sector can. But it's hard to see how the private sector can do a worse job than the government is doing.

For example:

The federal government sets safety standards for nuclear power generators. I was a member—a *pro-nuclear* member—of the congressional task force assigned to investigate the accident at Three Mile Island. Federally licensed operators working in a federally certified reactor plant, following federal standards, watched as computer typewriters fouled up, water levels in the reactor dropped with no reliable measuring gauge to tell the operators what was happening, relief valves stuck with no indicator to tell operators whether the valves were open or closed. A dangerous hydrogen bubble formed, but the operators didn't know what was happening. Radioactivity escaped. The government now admits there may be additional cancer deaths in the years to come among persons who live near the reactors.

The federal government set the standards for safety at nuclear processing plants like the Kerr-McGee facility near Crescent, Oklahoma. During courtroom testimony in the Karen Silkwood contamination case security officials admitted that large amounts of plutonium (they didn't know how much) had disappeared from the plant.

On another occasion plutonium disappeared (from another facility) and apparently ended up in another country. Plutonium, of course, is one of the materials used in building nuclear weapons.

The government is also in charge of air safety. Including the safety of DC-10 aircraft. How confident I feel as I drive to the airport, knowing that the federal government is making sure that nothing goes wrong. The FAA requires us to lock our seatbelts, put up our food trays, and stow our carry-on gear in an overhead rack or under the seat in front of us. And DC-10s fly with defects caused by faulty maintenance under the supervision of the federal government.

Government is in charge of our space program. It sent up the Skylab. What goes up must come down, we've always been told. But, not when what goes up goes into space, the government tells us. It goes around and around and around. But not the Skylab. It came down. Nice big chunks of it came down. The government thought it probably wouldn't hit anybody. We were lucky, after all; it didn't.

I know the government means well, but frankly I'd feel a little better if it didn't worry about me quite so much. With the government in charge of safety, who, I sometimes wonder, is in charge of disaster?

The great majority of members of Congress are as honest and as dedicated to their jobs as the great majority of people in any other walk of American life, whether running a bank or working on an assembly line. But even the most passionate defenders of the Congress have to admit that overall the record is not a good one.

Members of Congress may well be underpaid when one compares the rigorous nature of the job with most other jobs, or compares the extra living expenses incurred by Congressmen with the more routine expenses borne by their constituents—or even when one considers that the people who write the laws and oversee almost the entire federal government may earn one-tenth as much as people like Roman Polanski or Meatloaf. But maybe it can be argued (I offer this without comment) that people who sing silly songs well are deserving of more pay than people who run a country poorly.

The congressional pay raise of 1977 amounted to more than $13,000.

I simply could not accept it; we, as a Congress, had not done our job well.

I used most of that money to buy a small infant respirator for a suburban hospital and divided the rest between a children's hospital, a family service center and a home which provides care for children from broken homes.

To those who felt the money should have been returned to the treasury rather than to such charities, my answer was simple: the money belongs to the people who pay the taxes and not to the treasury which collects it from them. That's a point many in Washington have trouble with.

2. Social Awareness: Society Versus the Individual

Government *wants* to help; its compassion buds are bursting. We have become a nation blessed with the beneficence of thoughtful and kindly men who want to do us good, and there are no discernible limits as to how far they will go. We have spent millions on programs to study the mating calls of toads and require "Do Not Remove" labels for every pillow and mattress in the land.

Unfortunately, there seems to be no end to this great compassion coming out of Washington, and to some it seems rather unsporting of us to complain about it. There is, after all, a deep-rooted humanitarian spirit living in the chinks and cracks of the capital. From every corner, politicians accuse other politicians of a "lack of concern" for this group or that, and the accused respond with their own lists of people or things to which their accusers are insensitive. In order to prove their claim to the right to be entrusted with our national dream, politicians and non-elected intellectuals have adopted "humanitarianism" as the haircloth shirt of philosophical reality. "Sensitivity" is modern government's philosophical soup du jour, its presence in adequate amounts stoutly asserted and stiffly defended.

In this context, their sensitivity to the needs of others is proved by spending *your* money to benefit the group in question. It's called *vicarious* charity. Both Politician A and Politician B prove their sensitivity by spending somebody else's money.

Unfortunately, in their great rush to demonstrate their sensitivity to the needs of some, politicians are often insensitive to the needs of the many, those who provide the money with which they practice their charity.

Politicians who advocate expensive new spending programs sometimes seem to have no idea what the cost of that program will mean to the working man who will have to pay the bill, either through taxes or inflation. (For example, politicians who advocate expensive new national health insurance programs seem to forget that a man who earns $10,000 a year already works five times as long to pay his taxes as he does to pay for his health care bills, and that he could spend several times as much as he now does on health care or education or housing, if he were not forced to work more than a day and a half of each week to pay for federal programs.)

I do not merely dislike big government; I fear it. Throughout history the greatest obstacle to man's achievement of his dreams has been government. The history of man's progress, individually and collectively, has been the history of man's gradual achievement of greater freedom. Free men produce more, materially and intellectually. The greater the freedom, the greater the opportunity to make one's dreams come true.

In Taylor Caldwell's book *Great Lion of God*, Joseph says to Saul: "Was it not the Chinese who declared that governments are more to be feared than a tiger?"

Governments have destroyed many more people than tigers have.

It's time politicians demonstrated a sensitivity to the needs of those who give, not just of those who receive; to those who contribute as well as to those who benefit; to those who work, earn, and pay so the politician can demonstrate the goodness of his heart. Politicians often seem to have no understanding of how hard or how long a trucker, merchant, farmer, sales clerk or clown has to work to earn the money the "sensitive" politician proposes to take away from him.

It's time politicians demonstrated a sensitivity to the needs of *most* Americans—those Americans who give up part of their food, part of their clothing, part of their education, part of their health care, every time a "sensitive" politician decides to demonstrate his "sensitivity" by buying votes with somebody else's money.

There are several reasons for the emergence in modern politics of this peculiar 20th century humanism—this unhesitating willingness to spend somebody else's money for the good cause, no matter how much of that other person's money it takes (like the philanthropy of spirit-filled souls who write checks to charities on their corporate accounts).

One reason is philosophical. There are those who believe it is the proper function of government to redistribute what people have so nobody has more than anybody else. This redistribution would destroy all incentive to produce, and eventually there would be nothing left to distribute, but it's an honest opinion, sincerely held.

A second reason is this: It often costs a lot of money to get elected to public office in America and as a result, a disproportionate number of wealthy men and women serve in public office. Even if the Congress could limit what a candidate can put into his own campaign (it can't), candidates would still have to raise money and wealthy people can more easily raise money for campaigns. And because those who are not wealthy are understandably reluctant to give up a job in order to spend months campaigning, fewer people from the less affluent parts of society even entertain the idea of running for public office.

Many of the greatest contributions to American government have been made by men and women of great personal wealth, but their circumstances may nonetheless have a bearing on how they cast their votes as members of Congress. Wealthy men and women, like the less wealthy, may be truly concerned about the needs of the poor. There is this difference, however: a working man who is elected to Congress is far more likely to remember how it pinched every time the price of a pair of shoes or a loaf of bread went up, or how much it hurt when it came time to pay the taxes. The wealthy man may spend a great deal more, but simply cannot relate to the effect that paying for federal programs has on those who have to work hard to make ends meet. People who toss away $20,000 (or many times that) every year on travel, parties, or electronic gadgets simply cannot relate to the concerns of people who don't earn that much in a year and have to use every dollar they earn to feed, clothe, house and educate their families.

The well-to-do have probably been able to afford a better education, may have grown up in a family accustomed to community service, may be far better able to serve the country wisely and well than the less fortunate. And some of the wealthy members of Congress are also among the most conservative. But it would be foolish not to recognize that the larger number of wealthy people in public office, and the resultant "understanding gap" that often exists between them and their constituents, will sometimes be reflected in the votes they cast and the programs they support. It is one of the reasons for the big-spending Congresses of recent years.

And there is a third factor.

Many of today's politicians—and many of today's young people—take pride in thinking of themselves as idealists, as being part of a unique generation, more compassionate, more caring, more "concerned" than those that have gone before. And this concern, which is sincere and deeply held, is shared by the large number of younger members of Congress.

But if we are not to take everything at face value, is it not proper to ask: What *are* the ideals to which today's young politicians are devoted? To *what* do they direct their cares and concerns? To *what* are they dedicated?

A few years ago, the dean of student affairs at Harvard Medical School was quoted as saying that today's young medical student has a greater sense of "social awareness" than his medical predecessors. At the same time, however, an Associated Press survey revealed that young physicians were rejecting private medical practice in large numbers to enter public service, presumably because in that way they felt they could best express their "social awareness." A survey of 42 interns and residents at one Boston hospital revealed that none of the 42 planned to enter private medical practice. Another survey of graduating seniors at three Boston medical schools failed to turn up a single student who intended to enter private medical practice. Yet private practice is that branch of medicine in which doctors most directly care for people.

"Social awareness" refers to a concern for the well-being of a society. And society, as too many young liberals forget, is nothing more than a composite of individual beings.

What we have is a concern for "The People," without a corresponding concern for the individual. Concern for "The People" as an abstract mass, but not for the sick and afraid child; for the feeble old man; the shaking, lonely and fearful people who come one at a time for medical help—or who try to figure out how they are going to pay their taxes and still put food on the table.

Politicians tend to forget that tax bills are not paid by computers; they are paid by people—young people who cannot move into a better or bigger home to accommodate a growing family because inflation has driven the cost of a new or older home out of the reach of most young people; older people who must sell their homes because inflation and taxes have made home ownership almost impossible for people on small, fixed incomes.

It is not enough to proclaim one's concern; one must also show it.

I'm reminded of Rusanov, the ailing bureaucrat in Solzhenitsyn's *Cancer Ward.*

"The Rusanovs loved the People, their great People. They served the People and were ready to give their lives for the People. But as the years went by they found themselves less and less able to tolerate actual human beings. . . ."

Theodore Roszak, describing Karl Marx, said, "Yet there is no sensitivity for the person—only for 'the people'."

Clearly we need to start thinking less in terms of "The People," or "society" and more in terms of people.

Those who advocate new federal programs invariably refer to what it costs "society" *not* to have such a program. Or how such a program would benefit "society." But the costs that matter are the costs to the *individuals* in that society; the benefits that matter are not benefits to society, but benefits to the *people* who live in that society. (This, of course, changes all the figures, because the cost of administering federal programs, building new federal buildings, printing new federal forms, paying new federal payrolls cannot easily be justified when they are included in the overall cost of the program and then weighed against the actual benefits to *real* people.)

Society is merely a concept. What is important is the individual person who is a constituent part of "society." But many in government transfer their priorities from the concrete to the abstract; they place "society" above its actual component parts (people) in importance. In so doing, they ascribe to "society," an inanimate entity, human characteristics it does not possess—and they ignore the very real human beings in that society and how they are affected.

Government programs cannot cost "society" anything, for society has no money. It earns no money and can spend none. Only the individuals who make up society can earn or spend money. (Even government has no money. It can only take money from its individual citizens and redistribute it.)

The concept that society is more important than people is what permits acceptance of the view that money which is earned by individual citizens is properly the property of the government and that the citizen is entitled only to that portion which is left to him after taxes. (This argument is often used to oppose tax credits on the grounds that it is a government subsidy to allow a citizen to keep his own money.)

Compassion and concern are *personal* feelings—feelings individual people have for other individual people. It is this that is missing in the "social awareness" so prevalent in federal policy. One of the great challenges of today is to address the tremendous reservoir of idealism in the country and redirect its concerns from "The People" to individual people.

Politically, the result will be a *broader* sense of compassion—a concern for both the recipient *and* the giver (the taxpayer), an attempt to find what Walter Lippmann has called a balance between what is desired and what can be done.

Clearly, it is one of our great challenges to address the reservoir of idealism in America and redirect its concerns from "The People" to the people. That, however, becomes a question of prevalent philosophy, and to that extent Kafka is as much a part of the political debate in America as James Watt and the late-night news.

The drive for bigger and more powerful government is based on the concept that man is a helpless victim of life and must be protected by society. This is also the basic concept of one branch of literary existentialism, a philosophy which views life as basically absurd and hopeless; which views man as alienated, uprooted, helplessly entrapped in circumstance. And this, although we are breaking away from it, has been the basic political and social philosophy of the intellectuals and politicians of the mid-twentieth century.

This is not a philosophy of the distant past; one need not go back even so far as Camus' *The Stranger* or Sartre's *The Age of Reason*, both of which were written during the past 30 years. One can find it in recent movies ("Hair" is a good example; Berger, as he files into the troop transport to be flown overseas to his death, is at one with the doomed Meursault in "The Stranger" or Pablo in Sartre's "The Wall.")

This so-called "modern" philosophy holds that life is a succession of tragedies or, at best, of meaningless episodes; that the citizen is trapped in a series of events over which he has no control and in which he is only a spectator to the determination of his fate.

In the literature of this modern "realism," lovemaking is purely physical—and meaningless; there are no heroes and few victories; the goal is escape and the tools of escape are often marijuana, angel dust and cocaine.

The *political* extension of such a philosophy of life is a conviction that people are victims of circumstance, helpless to provide for their own well-being; that society must therefore protect its citizens against the vicissitudes of life. Not only does existentialism offer a convenient excuse for mistakes (or crime)—"I couldn't help it"—it also offers a political philosophy: the benevolent, protective government. To that extent, the political struggle, philosophically, has become one between those who believe man generally is incapable of meeting life's challenges and those who believe in the ability of man, under most circumstances, to regulate his own life. (Obviously there are people in unfortunate circumstances for whom government should properly provide; today's movies, books and plays depict people and circumstances that undoubtedly exist. The problem is in the assumption of universality.)

Implicit in the acceptance of responsibility for providing for others is the need for confidence in one's own ability to know the right answers—to know, for example, what is good for Citizen A; to know, without doubt, that *your* prescription for his happiness is correct. Otherwise one would lack the courage to implement a system that forces Citizen A to follow the planner's plan and not his own. (It was this "courage" that once prompted Ralph Waldo Emerson to complain: "A man who cannot be acquainted with me . . . ordains that a part of my labor shall go to this or that whimsical end—not as I, but as he happens to fancy.")

The problem is simply that the wise man must on occasion admit that he knows less than there is to know; that a given problem may be more complex that it at first appears.

That however, requires a degree of honesty rarely seen. (Irving Kristol once defined an intellectual as "a man who speaks with general authority about a subject on which he has no particular competence.")

Unfortunately, fast and simplistic answers—political shooting from the hip, a sport at which modern liberals are well practiced, are all too common. Easy answers are offered for the problems of mankind; simple solutions for the accumulated ills of the centuries.

The doctrine of *caveat emptor* can be easily extended to the buyer of ideas as well as the buyer of goods. We would be wise not to buy the day's political rhetoric too quickly.

An example comes to mind: the political debate over the environment.

The ecologists say that the streams, rivers and lakes of America are dangerously polluted, that the air is unfit to breathe, that the streets and sidewalks and even the parks are littered and unclean. Who can argue that is untrue? It is an accurate picture, certainly in the more heavily populated parts of the country.

Likewise, the Malthusians cry that our neighbors are pressing in on us from all sides, that the land cannot grow the necessary food, the cities cannot make room for housing, cannot provide transportation, cannot provide work, etc.

Without accepting such time-worn cliches as the "population explosion" (in fact, the population in some age groups is now beginning to decline, resulting in empty classrooms and school buildings—an altogether different problem), it is obvious that recent population growth has brought a need for increased housing, increased food supply, increased supplies of consumer goods, additional transportation facilities.

But now that the concerned have managed to get us all nodding our heads in unison and saying "yes," let's not follow them into the dialectic twist whereby they suddenly proclaim conclusions which perhaps deserve "no."

There seems to be an essential difference in the thought processes of the liberal (i.e., the advocate of governmental action) and the conservative or libertarian. The former often thinks with his heart and not his head; his sentiments are at the root of his conclusions, and he is thus likely to forget the basic necessity of checking his own premises and evaluating his "obvious" solutions.

The liberal sees a problem and proceeds forthwith to propound the most direct and pragmatic solution to the problem—the one which he deems will work most rapidly to erase the evil, regardless of the cost or any other impediments. The same people who cry for pharmaceutical manufacturers to state a drug product's contraindications and side effects in detail are often oblivious to the contraindications and side-effects of their own proposals in other areas.

The course of the conservative or libertarian is usually more deliberate, giving rise to the charge that he is unconcerned (a charge that, unfortunately, is occasionally true). The conservative seeks solutions which will not impinge on a citizen's freedoms and which will take into account the ramifications of a proposed new law or regulation. He will concern himself with whether or not the course proposed is one which is constitutionally permissible (an outdated concern among some liberals), and whether the long-range side effects will do more harm than the immediate good envisioned by the advocates.

How does this difference in approach find expression in the current environmental concerns?

The answers proposed by the self-proclaimed ecologist are usually simple and direct: federal control, federal restriction. Seldom does he propose tax incentives, for example, to encourage industry to devise means of continuing its amazing output of consumer goods while cleanly disposing of the waste generated by such production (although industry has solved other problems of awesome magnitude). Here the extreme environmentalists run head-on into their more general philosophies, which include a distrust of business and a reluctance to increase corporate income even if spent for a good cause. Plainly, the industrialists are the villains of the piece, and there will be no putting the fox in charge of the chicken coop.

(Let me add here that I have an almost equally strong disdain for some modern corporate executives, many of whom seem to lack both social conscience and political philosophy. Many corporations, in fact, represent the ultimate in pragmatic prostitution, sleeping with whoever will keep the competition at bay.)

The modern Malthusians similarly restrict their imaginations. They offer the same simplistic answers—limit family size, put the government in charge of providing housing, and so on. Thomas Malthus has been dead for more than 140 years. Long ago he predicted that we were all doomed to starvation and poverty because the arithmetical increases in means of subsistence would be far outdistanced by the geometrical increases in population. His deadline date for our doom has long since passed, but like the man with the sandwich-board who proclaims "The World is Coming to an End," the modern Malthusians think nothing of constantly changing the date of impending doom.

Their simplistic answers ignore the fact that as population grows, man has devised new ways of feeding himself. Today the once-arid desert yields sustenance to the determined Israelis; factories churn out artificial foods; the sea offers new frontiers of farming; engineers and architects devise new means of housing more for less.

But let me not offer simplistic answers myself. I am no expert on the complexities of such problems. I do know, though, that we must consider carefully all the effects of the solutions proposed to our problems and beware of following rhetoric into the dangerous and deep water of regulation and control.

CHAPTER FIVE
DREAMING DREAMS,
SETTING LIMITS

1. Creating the Society We Want to Live In

There are two questions all of us in public life should ask ourselves. The first is: *What kind of society, do we want to live in?*

And the second is: *What, if anything, should the government do to help bring that kind of society about?*

Unfortunately, those questions are so basic, the answers so understood, apparently, that no one bothers to ask them.

What kind of society *do* we want to live in?

If I were to ask myself that question, I would say this:

A society that respects the rights of people—all people—*as people.* A society that cares about people not as numbers or categories or colors or statistics, but as themselves. A society in which *we* matter.

In 1971, Kurt Vonnegut, the American novelist, gave a speech to the National Institute of Arts and Letters. In that speech he said the most satisfying teacher he had ever known was Dr. Robert Redfield, the head of the Department of Anthropology at the University of Chicago. Dr. Redfield, he said, dreamed about a society in which behavior would be "personal, not impersonal."

It would be a society in which people would think of other people as "myself in another form."

In such a society, he said, people would not deal impersonally with other people, as though they were things.

As simple as it sounds, it would be a great change from today's massive, impersonal society in which people become numbers designed to make computers work better.

Government, which could do so much to make things better usually makes things worse, and one of the main reasons for that is simply that too many people in government don't care about the rest of us. They are greatly concerned about us as a mass, as a "society," as numbers, as statistics—but not as people. There is no greater need in the world today than a government that is sensitive to the fears and the hopes and the goals and the ambitions and the prayers of the people it is supposed to serve.

Government *can* do good instead of harm. But to do good it has to care about us.

A number of years ago, Albert Jay Nock said he thought it would be interesting to write an essay on the subject of "How One Can Tell One is Living in a Dark Age".

So far as I know, he never wrote that essay. But maybe I have an answer. Maybe we're living in a Dark Age when we put things and society and government ahead of people.

What kind of society *do* we want to live in?

It's the most basic question any politician will ever face, yet neither conservatives not liberals ever address the *whole* question.

Conservatives tend to back into the question. They say, "in order to explain what kind of society I want to live in, first I have to tell you what kind of society I *don't* want to live in."

For example, conservatives don't want a society that goes too far in taking away its citizens' freedoms, or a society that takes away too much of what they earn, or a society that has too much regulation or always has inflation because it can't balance its budgets.

By defining what sorts of things we want to avoid in society, conservatives establish limits on what the government may do.

The problem is, after they define what they *don't* want government to do, conservatives often forget to go back and decide what they *do* want it to do. They sometimes forget to have any dreams, any visions of a better society.

Liberals, on the other hand, approach it from the other direction.

They dream dreams; they ask what kind of society they want, and they can see it—see it out there just beyond their fingertips, beckoning to them. And so they pursue the dream, without asking what kind of society they *don't* want (the question that sets limits).

Very few people who call themselves liberals actually want to take away peoples' freedoms—in fact most of them prize liberty just as much as the rest of us do—they just forget to ask what the consequences are going to be if they follow the first grand idea that comes into their minds to solve the problems that need solving.

Let me use an example:

A number of young children have died or been seriously injured because their pajamas caught fire, usually because they were standing too close to an open heater. The solution the government came up with was to order all pajama manufacturers to begin treating pajamas with a flame retardant. Later it was learned that the flame retardant causes cancer.

Another example:

Massive doses of saccharin, fed to laboratory animals, caused cancer. Because of an earlier law passed by the Congress, the FDA ordered saccharin taken off the market. Later, testimony before the Congress indicated that a great many people were dying from heart disease. Obesity was one of the villains. Saccharin, which had been removed from the market, was an important part of the fight against obesity. Eventually, Congress lifted the ban on saccharin.

Another example:

One of the dreams liberals have is a dream I share: a dream of a clean environment, with air you can breathe and water you can drink and beautiful scenery you can walk through.

Another of the dreams I have is this: more jobs, so more people can work, and so more of them can share in the kind of good life most of us have.

The problem is, to have the second of those dreams come true, we must have energy to keep our businesses and factories going. That means we need to have more oil and gas now, and later other kinds of energy.

But in pursuit of our mutual desire to take care of the environment, a lot of liberals have stopped any kind of drilling or mining that would produce more energy, and so during cold winters plants close down, schools close, a few people in the cold northeast freeze to death in their rooms, companies can't expand so there are no new jobs for people who don't have them.

Sometimes liberals seem to care more about the environment than they care about the people who use it. Sometimes liberals treat trees like people and people like trees.

Liberals also forget to ask what things cost. They're like people who walk around writing checks and forget to write the amounts down in their checkbooks. One must be rich, though, to do that, and the

United States is not. We take in something more than half a trillion dollars a year in taxes. By 1980, we had accumulated liabilities, obligations and commitments of more than ten and one-half trillion dollars. That means we've already spent 21 times what we take in in one year. We're committed for almost the next quarter of a century.

There are sides to this box:

Liberals see the problems, but their solutions are awful. Sometimes their cures are worse than the disease.

Too many conservatives never see the problems at all.

Let me state the obvious:

We need politicians with the sensitivity of liberals in being able to see the problems: there *are* places where the air is so foul you can choke on it, and places where the water is so putrid you can't drink it. There *are* a lot of people who don't have jobs and can't get them, and people who live in houses and apartments with leaky roofs or are beset by rats.

And we need politicians who have the conservative's sense of limits to what government can do without making *everybody* miserable in trying to help the few who are miserable now.

Those two viewpoints seem to me to set the boundaries for establishing what kind of a government we ought to have. Between those two outer barriers—the need to come up with solutions on the one hand, the need to preserve freedoms and not take away all we earn on the other—government can be made to work.

There is no question that these conclusions are simple. And yet, simple as they are, one need only spend some time with either conservatives or liberals (and in the Congress I spend much time with both) to learn that while these few conclusions may be both simple and obvious, not many people seem to have thought of them.

While it may seem a simple enough thing to think and say, it is assuredly *not* a simple thing to put into practice.

Liberals are not *used* to first asking themselves "what constraints must I put on myself in attempting to seek solutions to this problem?"

And conservatives are not used to saying to themselves: "how can I work within the free enterprise system—or use some government incentive to *steer* that system—to solve the problems I see."

The conservative will at first respond to this suggestion by saying, "We believe in free enterprise; we oppose federal regulation; we don't want the federal government to come in and tell businesses that they have to do things, even if those things should be done."

Conservatives must learn to say: "here's the problem; I see it; here are the limits to what *government* should do; how can we solve the problem within those limits?" It is simply not enough to hope the problems will just go away.

There are ways in which government does legitimately deal with people in business. There are disagreements as to *the amount* businesses should be taxed, but *some* level of taxation is proper. So why can we not approach the problem in this way:

We can agree that it is our desire that workingmen have a safer place to work.

We can create a million regulations ordering businessmen to show their employees how to climb ladders. We *can* create an agency to fine and punish businessmen who do not comply with those regulations.

Or we can tell businessmen we want their workers to have a safe and healthy place to work, and while it is proper that we take some money from that business in taxes, and we will continue to do so, the businessman can keep a portion of what he would have paid in taxes if, instead of putting that money in his pocket, he uses it to improve safety and health conditions for his employees.

The result would be the same: healthy and safe places for people to work.

And the rest of us won't have to pay the taxes to support OSHA and its army of inspectors, and we won't have to pay the higher prices for his products that would result when the businessman increased prices to pay for the added expense of complying with the regulations.

Sure, the government would be taking in less money in taxes and it can be argued that we'll have to make up the difference. Why? The taxes went to pay for OSHA and its offices and its forms and its filing cabinets and its inspectors and their pencils and their automobile expenses and the like.

Now, I should add that the issue is clearly more complex than the simplification I have given here. There would be inspections, probably, to make sure the improvements were actually made, so IRS would have to determine whether its current force of inspectors would be adequate to check on the tax credits claimed by those businessmen who improved working conditions for their employees.

Many of these solutions will require a great deal of legislative consideration. But solutions *can* be found—we can solve problems and still remain sensitive to the needs of *all* the people, including the need to preserve their freedoms and to leave as much of their money as possible in their pockets, to be used in pursuit of their own goals, to make their own dreams come true.

The purpose of politics is to create the society we would all like to live in.

I think that society would have a great degree of privacy for anybody who wanted it.

People would have access to a good education.

People would have access to jobs—*good* jobs. Jobs that offer challenge and enjoyment, and that would offer some opportunity to enjoy life and set something aside for later. (Artificial jobs created by the government are "dead-end" jobs that last a little while and then disappear. It is in the private workplace that we find the kinds of jobs I'm talking about, and we need to have more of them.)

People would have enough access to cheap energy to be able to enjoy some of the luxuries of life.

The society would be free from war. There are, of course, different viewpoints on how to achieve that ideal situation. Some liberals—the ones who not only enjoyed the movie "Camelot," but thought it was a true story (in Camelot they simply outlawed things like rain and snow)—have a great solution to this problem: Dismantle all our guns and burn our uniforms and since our enemies won't have anybody to fight with any more, there will be no more war. Others think the best way to keep from having a war is to be strong enough that nobody will want to pick a fight.

There are good and not-so-good ways to try to make this dream world come true. In Kenya, which has a private enterprise system, there is a great deal of abundance and prosperity. In socialist Tanzania, right next door, things are not so good.

The important point is this: Governments are created by the people, not the other way around; governments should help people achieve *their* goals, not the other way around. The combined efforts of all of us—combined by establishing a government—should be directed toward making this kind of society come true.

When the first immigrants came to the United States—and later, in the 1890s and early 1900s, when hundreds of thousands more followed—it was commonly believed they were coming to this country looking for streets of gold. I think people misunderstood what they meant. They did not believe the United States was so richly endowed with natural resources, easily obtained, that the paving stones in the streets were 14 karat. The streets were golden *because of where they led*. And where they led was just about anywhere anybody wanted to go. They were open-ended lanes and streets, without artificial barriers at the end, saying this goal is off-limits.

That was not quite true, of course. There *were* barriers, but for the most part they existed in spite of our laws and our basic beliefs, not because of them, and we have spent some 200 years knocking those barriers down, some very quickly and others a great deal more slowly, but knocking them down nonetheless. And in the meantime, many people who were at dead ends in their old countries came here and made it big. (Some became very rich, of course, but that's not what I mean by making it "big." I mean that in most cases their children or grandchildren have comfortable homes and jobs and clothes and now *their* grandchildren can get an education and can enter almost any career or profession that appeals to them. A small achievement? Not for many of the people who came here. Not a small achievement at all.)

What do I mean when I say that government should help achieve the kind of society we want, and not the other way around?

I mean that *government should not be a barrier to achieving that kind of society.*

Government *can* be a barrier. Often it is. It was a barrier in Youngstown, Ohio, for example. In one way or another, in Youngstown, government policies played a major role in tossing thousands of steel workers out of work.

Another example:

We all want clean air, and the Environmental Protection Agency has set standards to ensure that air will be kept clean. These standards, however, are so strict that for some cities they have meant a virtual halt to economic growth. When General Motors decided to move an assembly plant to Oklahoma City, for example, city officials had to work for months to find a way to clean up the city's already clean air because the addition of the GM plant would have increased pollution above the EPA's acceptable standards, even though Oklahoma City has virtually no pollution problem whatsoever. A number of companies already in Oklahoma City made costly overhauls to cut back on their own already low output of contaminants, and the GM plant was eventually opened, providing thousands of jobs for Oklahoma workers. But unless such standards are changed, Oklahoma City and many other cities like it may have reached a dead end which will mean no new jobs.

Despite our great efforts in this country to achieve an economic system that benefits all people, there are still haves and have-nots. The essential difference is this: what the haves have are jobs in private enterprise; what the have-nots don't have are jobs. To have a society that continues to provide opportunity for upward mobility we have to have jobs, and government, with its various no-growth policies, is a major roadblock for those who are still trying to make it into the system.

We need laws that require federal agencies to study the impact of their regulations on the creation of new jobs (or the elimination of old ones), and laws that require an analysis of the cost of complying with federal regulations.

In short, we need laws that require the government itself to take actual people into account, and what the effect of the government's policies will be on those people. That would be a radical change in the way our government goes about its business, but it's a change that's long overdue.

2. The Greatest Crime: Wasting Human Potential

This is the greatest crime a society can commit: *To rob a man of his future.*

It is a crime that can be carried out in many ways.

In "Where the Wasteland Ends" Theodore Roszak wrote of the poet William Blake: "He saw in the steady advance of science and its machines a terrifying aggression against precious human potentialities."

Studs Terkel, in *Talking to Myself*, described an interview he had with British stage director Joan Littlewood: "I'd like to see people realize their full height," she said. "But in life, there's a disaster all the time. The waste of human possibility."

The late Harry Chapin composed a song about a young boy whose imagination sees in the beauty of the rose all the colors of the rainbow, and it is with that artistic vision that he performed his classroom drawing assignments. The child's teacher insists that the drawing is unacceptable: "Roses are red," she says, and "the color of the leaves is green." Heaven only knows, and Chapin did not tell us, what she might have said to Monet. Eventually the boy responds to what he is taught; he can no longer see any color in the rose and its leaves but red and green.

America must commit itself to preserving potential.

Society commits so many aggressions against human potential, wastes so many human possibilities. Society commits this crime not only against its members individually, but collectively as well—against itself as the beneficiary of man's achievements.

And it commits these aggressions in many ways.

It is easy, of course, to visualize how that potential is destroyed in the more extreme cases. War, for example, is the world's single greatest mass destroyer of human potential. In the Broadway play, "Hair," when we learn that Berger has been killed in Vietnam, after we have hear him sing and watched him dance, our reaction is more than mourning for what was; it is also a sadness for what will not be.

When we are first exposed to the sensitivity that moved Joyce Kilmer to write: "I think that I shall never see a poem lovely as a tree," and then learn of his death in a war; when we learn of Alan Seeger's "rendezvous with death," the sorrow we feel is not only because of the death of somebody who created beauty, but because of the potential that has been destroyed, the beauty that will not be created.

But more people continue to live, despite wars, than die in wars. And so the question becomes: what of the things society does to destroy the human potential of those who do *not* die in war.

A case can be made for war against the Hitlers who come like the plague, and maybe the futures destroyed in those wars are a necessary sacrifice to keep the world going on a reasonably sane course.

But what case can be made for the teacher in Harry Chapin's song?

What case can be made for the laws, and the prejudices, that deny access to arts, trades, professions, futures because somebody is the "wrong" sex, the "wrong" color, speaks with the "wrong" accent, or practices the "wrong" religion?

What case can be made for an educational system that fails to provide children with the basic skills they need to succeed in life?

An unfeeling society can crush more than lives: it crushes imagination, opportunity, hope, dreams, futures.

It is not enough merely to "love" one another; it is also mandatory to allow each individual to become all that he or she can be.

Are all roses red? Are red roses only red?

How many Renoirs had their visions knocked out of them by a society that worshipped only Rembrandt? (For that matter, how many Benny Goodmans had their clarinets taken away when they began to experiment with jazz?)

In even the most tolerant society, there is no room for an architect who dreams majestic dreams but was not taught math.

An even the man with a better mousetrap will never achieve business success if he is turned away by lenders because he is the wrong color.

There is another point that ought to be made.

If it is important to ask what kind of society we want to live in, it is no less important to understand fully what kind of society we want *not* to live in.

Liberty is the sunshine of the soul, and there are places where the sun doesn't shine.

There is a portrait of Patrick Henry on my office wall and a drawing of Chief Joseph. They remind me of why I'm in Washington. There are photographs: photographs of starving families and makeshift shacks; of grime-covered children emerging from the breakers of the coal mines; of blacks, their backs laced with scars from a master's whip. There are pictures of my own children who will live in the world we leave them. They are reminders, too.

They are not the only reminders.

There's a small statue of Snoopy and Woodstock on my desk. Woodstock has a flag with a question-mark on it. On the base of the statue are these words. "He's a nice guy but I don't know where he stands."

I have a small paperweight, given to me after my election by two campaign workers. It says simply: "Don't forget the little taxpayers."

I have a plastic bottle of aspirin marked "For Potomac Fever" ("Potomac Fever" is what they call it when you forget the folks back home).

And on the wall are two other things: a map tracing the more than 50,000 homes I visited during the 1976 campaign and a reminder of why I did it—a haunting color photograph which ties all these pieces together. It is a rather ordinary scene: a kitchen table with a small desk-top calendar, a bowl of flowers; a portrait of life. But these are only hints of life. There is no human life to be seen, and it is thus also a portrait of human emptiness and loneliness and a great, almost unbearable, sadness.

It is a portrait that could have been taken in Oklahoma City, or for that matter anywhere in America. But is precisely the fact that the photograph was not taken in Oklahoma City, not taken in America, that ties the pieces together in a portrait not of a kitchen table but of common humanity and the universal and eternal cry for freedom that is the central focus of all politics.

The photographer, whom I have never met, is a man I may never meet. His name is Isaac Zlotver. He is a Russian, a Jew, a *Refusenik*, a man whose sole remaining hope in life is that he may leave Russia, that he may see Israel, that he may openly practice the religion of his fathers; that he may freely travel.

But if that day comes, Isaac Zlotver will travel alone. His wife no longer shares his dream, his unspeakable yearning for freedom. She is dead—dead in Russia, dead without knowing the freedom she so desperately wanted. What greater misery is there than to lie on one's deathbed denied the dream of a lifetime? Mrs. Zlotver was alive when her husband took the photograph that hangs in my office; perhaps she stood at his side as he pressed the shutter; perhaps she arranged the flowers. Surely she shared the hope that in carrying this tiny message to an American Congressman somehow the dream might come closer to reality.

Liberty, like most things, is most precious to those without it. Blessed with freedom, American liberals willingly surrender it in small chunks to pursue other goals, other aspirations. But once liberty is gone, it cannot easily be regained. The goals liberals pursue are proper goals for humane men living in society with one another—the sharing of opportunity, widespread education and universal good health. Their mistake is to think that those goals are best reached by sacrificing liberty; in fact, the opposite is true. A free society provides more bread and more people share in eating it.

It is true, of course, that an abstract principle, even one so dear as liberty, speaks in muted tones to men without food in their bellies. And yet countless runaway slaves in the period of this country's immaturity attest to the powerful magnet freedom is, even when the alternative is a benevolent master and a full plate.

If the Soviet Union cannot match the Western world in providng its citizens with the luxuries of life, or even most of the necessities in very great abundance, it is nevertheless true that an honest, hard-

working Soviet citizen can feed and clothe his family and live in relative comfort by non-Western standards. Those like Zlotver, Sinyavsky,
Solzhenitsyn, Scharhansky, Karpov and thousands of others who have
left the Soviet Union, or gone to prison camps within it, have done so
not for bread but for a deeper kind of sustenance. Whether to write or
to worship or to walk in a freer air, they have risked much—and sometimes all—for freedom.

The American Indian, pressed back from his own lands, confined
to foreign lands, restricted in his movements, knew the same hunger.
Chief Joseph, too, cried for liberty. But Joseph, and Red Cloud, and
Modock Jack, and the Cherokees, and the Choctaws, and the tribes of
the south and the west, lost their liberty, too.

Politics is always a battle between those who seek more freedom
and those who seek to reduce it. That is all politics is. It will always be
the same. It was so when Moses served the Pharaoh and when he left
the Pharaoh; when Tolstoi wrote in Russia; when the Athenians debated; when the Spartans debated; when the Romans debated; when
the first tribal chieftains gave their orders in the caves of pre-history.

There are extremes and excesses; resistance that leads to war and
resistance that melts into surrender; tyrants and kindly kings. But the
central issue remains the same in every age and in every country, and it
is this one: on the one hand those who ask, "Does this maximize freedom, or lessen it; does this recognize man as a free being; does this preserve man's right to live his own life?" and on the other, those who
say, "Freedom is a value, but other values are even greater and freedom
must be surrendered that other good may follow."

Those who seek to limit freedom, to constrain it, do so often for
the best, the most humane, of reasons. It has always been thus with
every strong government of the right or the left, for few men, if any,
openly admit even to themselves a simple psychological thirst for
power, or even a belief in their own superior wisdom and ability to
manage others' lives. Hitler deprived Germans of freedoms to preserve
the fragile web that supported the great dream of a strong and pros-
perous Germany; Mao did it to modernize a backward rural giant;
Franco did it; Tito did it; Russians and Iranians and South Africans
and Cubans suppress freedom and never fall short on excuses.

I submit that Isaac Zlotver will not be easily swayed by such philosophical theorizing.

The Isaac Zlotvers of the world lose their civil rights—their human
rights—because too many stand by while Hitler murders; while Rus-

sian tanks roll over Hungary and Poland and Czechoslovakia and Afghanistan; while Cambodians and Ugandans are slaughtered; while American blacks are lynched or denied the right to enter public schools or vote in elections.

And they lose their rights, too, because too many in governments around the world forget the taxpayers—the peasant or the worker or the housewife whose money is taken, whose dreams are taken, whose freedom is taken to support the machinery of government that keeps grinding out good but somehow ends up doing the most good, in each society, for those who run the government.

I mentioned something else on my office wall, something else that describes why I have come here, behind enemy lines:

It's a wall map. A map of the streets and side streets I walked to get to Washington. For nearly a year, in rain and in Oklahoma heat, I walked from house to house, to 50,000 houses in all. I did it to participate in something Isaac Zlotver has never known. A free election. Totally free. People who wanted to say or write unpleasant things about me did. People who wanted to help me did. I was free to go to strangers' homes and talk politics with them, to urge them to change their government. I did what people in other parts of the world are forbidden to do. I did what men have died for. I did what Americans take for granted, but what an Isaac Zlotver would probably be executed for.

And so Isaac Zlotver's photograph, that photograph that hangs on my wall and goes unnoticed by visitors to my office, is a link from Russia, today, to the eternal cry of Patrick Henry, of Chief Joseph, of Moses, to governments everywhere, in all ages, to let the people go, to let them pursue their own goals and dreams.

And that is why, as we dream our dreams of what we hope will be, we must also remember what was, what is and what must never be. Just as the good society includes things, it also excludes things. And so the first thing it must exclude is government so big, so powerful, so distant, so uncaring, that it works against, not for, the people.

This was taken during a meeting with the President in the White House. I was there as a member of the Republican Whip organization, which marshals support for Republican legislation in the House. The next term I was promoted to Regional Whip, with responsibility for 12 Western states. The other two Congressmen in the picture are John Napier, of South Carolina, who was defeated a few months later, and Vin Weber, of Minnesota.

Jim Buckley, a former Senator from New York (and Bill Buckley's brother), became Undersecretary of State in the Reagan Administration before moving on to run Radio Free Europe. This picture was taken during a meeting in my office when Jim called on me to try to persuade me – as a member of the Foreign Operations subcommittee – to support the Administration's foreign aid bill. I believe we need to make major changes in our foreign assistance program and explained that I couldn't support foreign aid programs until some basic policies were changed. They weren't and I voted against the bill.

During my second term in the House I was the ranking member of the Health and Safety subcommittee. Here, I'm meeting with Paul Dwyer, the committee's chief counsel, during a break between committee witnesses.

As chairman of the American Conservative Union I was also chairman of the annual Conservative Political Action Conference which draws close to 2,000 political activists – and staunch Reagan supporters – to Washington every winter. At the moment this was taken I was urging the President – not very successfully, I'm afraid – to declassify some of the information we have about the extent of the Soviet military buildup. The Pentagon and the State Department are afraid to let the Soviets know how much we know. The man in the back (behind the President) is Terrell Bell, the Secretary of Education, who later rose to new prominence in the Administration when the education issue moved to the top of the public agenda. The beard, by the way, lasted for only three months and was grown because I wanted to compare my own appearance with some old photos of my father, who grew a beard each year for Oklahoma's annual celebration of the Run of 1889. My constituents hated the beard. Some thought it meant I was becoming a liberal; maybe others just thought it made me even uglier. At any rate, it came off in a hurry, a concession to political realities.

I've enjoyed a good relationship with the Vice President for some time now, although I worked actively for the Reagan campaign in 1980. Once, George (when he was still just George) passed me in the Capitol. I recognized him, but he didn't know me from Adam. One of his staff people whispered to him and he came back to me and said, "Mickey! It's good to see you again." I was very impressed – not that he remembered me (we had never met) but that he had such good staff work. This, by the way, is in the Vice President's office; my office doesn't have such fancy furniture.

During the Reagan campaign I was director of an advisory team made up of 20 individual task forces, each chaired by a Senator and a House member. This was at a meeting between the candidate and the chairman of the task forces, which had been set up to advise the Campaign on a wide range of national issues.

I met Ambassador Ruarz, third from the left, shortly after he defected from his post as the Polish ambassador to Japan in protest against the government's declaration of martial law. Being half-Polish myself (my father's parents were born just outside of Warsaw), I had a great sympathy for the problems Poles have had as a result of being sandwiched between – and dominated by – larger, more powerful neighbors for so many years. As chairman of the American Conservative Union I presented the Ambassador with an award at the annual Conservative Political Action Conference. Here we are in Jack Kemp's office, with the other Republican members of the Foreign Operations subcommittee. The others are John Porter, left, from the Chicago suburbs (John and his wife, Kathryn, are good friends of ours, and Lisa frequently calls on their daughters to baby-sit with Patrick); Jack Kemp, the leading spokesman for growth-oriented conservatism (and some of the ideas I echo in this book); Bob Livingston, from New Orleans, who, like me, has proven that conservatives can win black votes – although not if they had to listen to him trying to learn to play the trumpet – and Jerry Lewis, of California, who has become a leading critic of the World Bank and the International Monetary Fund.

The others, starting at the left, are John Porter, Jerry Lewis, and Bob Livingston. John moved to another subcommittee in the next session after the committee ratios were changed to reflect the seats we lost in the 1982 elections. (Actually, the Speaker stacked the committee ratios a little, and we lost more committee seats than we should have – but he had the votes and Tip thinks the minority party's only real function is to help make up a quorum.)

Senior citizens are increasingly affected by what the Congress does, and as a result more and more public attention is focused on the annual White House Conference on Aging, which deals with the issues which will confront the growing number of the aged. Here I'm meeting in my office with some of Oklahoma's representatives to the conference – Frank Buce, of Bartlesville, Bob and Martha Goldman, of Oklahoma City, and Joan Blankenship, of Tulsa. I finally decided that it was a conference to discuss issues of concern to the aged and not a conference of the aged. Frank Buce and I were active in the Young Republicans at the same time and I refuse to put either of us in the "aged" category yet, although he's already turned gray and I'm getting there.

In my second term, I put together a presentation on the House floor about the growing threat of Soviet control of the sea lanes. Here I prepare for the presentation with Rep. Gerry Solomon of New York.

Here I'm discussing the farm program with Agriculture Secretary John Block. The Administration's co-called ''PIK'' (payment-in-kind) program was well received the first time it was offered, but the Department of Agriculture had underestimated the number of farmers who would participate and the amount of wheat that would be needed, and the program ran into some strong criticism. The program was changed considerably in its second year, primarily to require farmers to take more land out of production, and the program was not accepted very enthusiastically.

Conservative protests about the size of the deficit in the President's proposed budget resulted in a so-called "Yellowjacket Revolt" (we were called "Yellowjackets" because we once sent notice of our displeasure by casting yellow "present" votes on a critical amendment), and resulted in our inclusion in the drafting of a revised budget which forced the deficit down by cutting spending. Here we're all doing a little figuring at a meeting with the President in the Cabinet Room at the White House. That's Bob Michel, the House Republican leader, between the President and me, and Del Latta, of Ohio, the ranking Republican on the House budget committee, on the other side of the President. In the background are Ed Rollins, the President's chief political assistant (with the beard) and Ken Duberstein, the chief White House liaison to the Congress.

During my second term in the House, I served as chairman of a Republican campaign to force the House leadership to permit votes on bills that had been introduced to reduce taxes. Here I'm at a press conference with Guy Vander Jagt, the chairman of the National Republican Congressional Committee, John Rhodes, then the House Republican leader, and at the right, Bob Michel, then the House Republican Whip.

The House Republican leadership asked me to head a campaign to call public attention to the large number of tax reduction bills that had been bottled up in House committees and prevented from coming to a vote. Here, I'm displaying a computer printout of bills that had been introduced but on which no action had been taken.

CHAPTER SIX
INSTITUTIONAL INSANITY:
BARNUM AND BAILEY ON THE POTOMAC

1. Saccharin, Sealing Wax, and a Presumption of Shadiness: Congress as an Obstacle

The Congress is in itself a significant institutional roadblock to sanity.

The Congress is in desperate need of change if it is to be responsive to the needs and desires of the American people.

The problem is not with the way in which the institution reacts, but with the institution itself.

In many ways the institution's internal structures are outdated, designed for a time when votes were fewer and the pace slower.

There are many reasons for this institutional breakdown: the overwhelming mass of issues to be debated and voted upon in every session of Congress (the result of a modern conviction that everything needs to be made law); rules which permit committees, subcommittees and the entire Congress to be in session at the same time; the ability of the House leadership to change the rules to permit major issues to be brought up with virtually no notice; a flexibility which leads to major issues coming to the floor in quick succession, piled one atop another, in a blinding flurry of debate and amendments stretching far into the night and—stretching for weeks or months before and after—long periods of virtual inactivity, with the House rarely in session and seldom voting on anything at all.

After years of studying political philosophy, economics, foreign affairs, a Congressman finds himself finally dealing with the immediate issues of the day—saccharin, air bags, metric conversion, tobacco subsidies, protecting whales and imposing import duties on sealing wax.

These issues, and important ones, are debated and weighed in modern America's version of an itinerant free-wheeling fast-moving tent-top clowns-bears-and wild Indians Barnum and Bailey circus.

At times, the congressional schedule moves like a turtle tiptoeing through a mass of molasses. In the first three and one-half months of the second session of the 97th Congress (that is, the first three and one-half months of 1982) the House of Representatives was in session for a total of 50 days, almost all of those sessions "pro forma" (a three-player comedy in which one calls the session to order, another—the chaplain—asks the Lord's blessings on that day's deliberations, and a third moves to adjourn). As the second-ranking Republican on the Foreign Operations Subcommittee I took a week off to go to Poland during that time (we were about to begin consideration of our response to the Polish government's declaration of martial law); during that week, seven days, top to bottom, morning and night, the seven members of the delegation missed only three votes, none of them of consequence.

In the last week of the 95th Congress, with elections getting closer and the legislative plate still full, the Congress got down to business. Significant money bills ("significant," in Congressional terms, meaning megabillions, millions being the minor stuff) and a major legislative package with awesome impact on energy production were heaped together, along with everything else the Rules Committee and the Speaker could drag from the refrigerator, and shoved in front of us.

On Wednesday before the final adjournment for the year the House convened at 10 o'clock in the morning. We adjourned for the night (for the morning, actually) at 1:30 or so the next morning (Thursday). We started in again at 10 a.m. on Thursday, and stayed in session until nearly 2 a.m. on Friday. We were back in session at 10 a.m. on Friday, debating, voting, considering, thinking, and stayed at it until 1:30 on Saturday morning. Saturday the House took off an extra two hours (until noon) so Members who wished to do so could attend funerals (one in Maryland, one in Chicago) of two Congressmen who had died in the midst of things. We were back in session at noon on Saturday and stayed in session until the plate was clean and everybody had burped (I participated in the energy debate; I spoke at 3 a.m. to a nearly empty chamber, while the audience I hoped to convince dozed in front of me, or, in much larger numbers, in the cloakrooms or their own offices.) The bells rang for votes at odd hours (once I noticed that Glenn English, who represents the district next to mine, had failed to show up for a vote; I called his office and woke him up. We spent most of the rest of the morning drinking coffee in the small dining room just below the House chambers). On and on it went, discussing, debating, disposing of energy bills, tax bills, spending bills, members fuzzy-headed from lack of sleep. We finished at 7 p.m. on Sunday, 31 hours after the Saturday session had started, and headed home to explain to the voters how well we had represented them and why we should be sent back for more.

There are other roadblocks to sanity as well.

One is the extent to which Members of Congress—especially members of the House, with its larger size and greater anonymity—tend to become lumped into a political aggregate and to be judged as a part of that aggregate.

It is not uncommon to be subjected to some rather colorful language merely because of my membership in the House of Representatives. It is apparently difficult sometimes to differentiate—especially from a distance—between those in the House who spend as though they were playing Monopoly and those who spend like Ebenezer Scrooge before he saw the ghost.

And it is equally difficult, apparently, to differentiate between those who are taking liberties with the public trust and those who are not. As a result, if one member of Congress is found drunk in the Tidal Basin, or five are trapped in the Abscam investigation, or several are known to have received money from the South Korean government, then the cloud of suspicion and distrust which descends covers alike both the guilty and the innocent. To be a member of Congress is to be presumed guilty of the lowest standards of human conduct simply because of those with whom one associates.

It is precisely this business of all being tarred with the same brush which has so diminished in the public view the integrity of its Congress. As a whole, the Congress is profligate; when it comes to spending the taxpayer's money, a full majority of the House has time and again shown itself unable to exercise even the slightest restraint.

In his book *Reclaiming the American Dream*, Richard Cornuelle said the Congress in shaping public policy should first know the following: "How many people are in trouble? Why? What are we already doing about it in all three sectors? What else should we be doing? Who should do it?'' Those questions, however, are seldom asked; instead the Congress simply attempts to do away with problems by tossing great amounts of money and federal regulation at them. And it does that by the votes of a majority of its members. Therefore, any criticism directed at the Congress for such habits is more justified (despite its unfairness to the minority who oppose such programs), than is automatic suspicion of a Congressman's honesty when, in fact, only a small percentage of the House has been shown to be guilty of anything and the rest must, under our system of justice, be presumed to be innocent.

Politically, however, it doesn't work that way. There is a presumption of shadiness hanging over the place. The shade of suspicion which attaches to membership in the Congress will undoubtedly continue to linger until the leadership in the House shows a greater willingness to tackle allegations forthrightly and get to the bottom of them. The Koreagate investigation, as it came to be called, fizzled to a close with a few meaningless slaps on repentant wrists. As soon as the House had done its meaningless scolding the scoldees were surrounded by sympathetic colleagues pounding them encouragingly on the back, and were permitted to rejoin the circle. Within the hour, all were again voting on the issues before the House as though nothing at all had happened.

A cartoon in the *Chicago Tribune* depicted inmates in a prison cell block. One says to another: "I went wrong by not following a youthful desire to serve in the U.S. Senate, where I would have only been denounced."

If the congressional leadership does not show a greater willingness to discipline breaches of the public trust, we may find ourselves as willing to admit membership in the Congress as to having spent the previous night in a brothel or at a chapter meeting of the KKK.

It doesn't matter a lot, actually, whether or not a Congressman knows what he is doing, because there's not enough time to do it anyway. The single greatest frustration for any member of Congress is the lack of time available for him to do the job he thought he was elected to do.

At one early briefing, even before taking the oath of office for the first time, I learned that a recent study had revealed that the average member of Congress has only about 11 minutes a day to read or think about the issues he is about to consider. That may be true. If it is, somebody else is getting my 11 minutes.

On Christmas Day in 1979, Alan Ehrenhalt, then a staff writer for the *Washington Star,* reported on rebellion brewing among younger members who were putting together a move to try to streamline procedures in the House.

> Republican Representative David Stockman of Michigan returned from participation in the 648th roll call vote of the year in the House repeating one of the chamber's most common complaints.
>
> "Problems are complex," he says, "and the legislative products being reported to the House are terribly shoddy and incomplete. And it's not due to the lack of ability on the part of the members. It's due to the schedule and the zoo-like atmosphere.
>
> Back in his office after the day's fourth dash to the House floor to vote...Democratic Representative Richard Gephardt of Missouri agrees.
>
> "We spend an incredible amount of energy transporting ourselves to the floor," he says. 'It's a total waste of time. One reason we don't have a consensus on more things is that we don't have time to think about them."

In addition to floor demands, the typical member of Congress serves on two committees and at least four subcommittees. I currently serve on the Appropriations Committee, one of three key House committees with such broad jurisdiction that its members are limited to a single committee assignment, but for the first four years I served in the House, I was a member of the House Interior Committee, two of its subcommittees—Energy and Environment (the most active) and National Parks—and the Education and Labor Committee, on which I was, when I left, the top-ranking Republican member of the Health and Safety Subcommittee and a member of two other subcommittees, Postsecondary Education and Labor Standards. In addition to those two committees and five subcommittees, I was chairman of a standing task force on regulatory reform, a member of a Republican strategy group, chairman of the Sunbelt Caucus, chairman of an informal luncheon group, and a participant in a host of other activities within both the House and the Republican Party's internal structure. (I am deliberately excluding other activities, outside the Congress—I am chairman of the American Conservative Union, a national grassroots lobbying organization with more than 325,000 members and active supporters—even though most members of Congress have involvements outside the Congress itself, involvements which help them achieve the goals which led us into Congress in the first place, and which also eat into valuable time.)

It is one of the frustrations of the office that the people we represent so often fail to understand the demands on our time and are quick to anger when we are unable to have lunch with them, attend their receptions or fly back to our hometowns to introduce the speaker at one of their weekly meetings.

Early in 1979, a constituent asked to visit me in Washington to discuss a problem his son-in-law was having in the Army. I agreed to the meeting, which was to take place the following week. At the appointed time, however, I found myself in the midst of a hearing, several buildings away, questioning an important committee witness. I called my office and arranged to have the constituent meet with my administrative assistant (the top member of the staff) and my senior legislative assistant. During my questioning of the committee witness the bells rang for a vote and I had to go to the House floor. I arrived in my office, finally, about 30 minutes late and then, with my two top assistants, spent nearly an hour meeting with the constituent and his son-in-law.

After he returned to Oklahoma City, the constituent wrote a pointed and unpleasant letter sharply criticizing me for not having been in my office on time to meet with him.

It's not an uncommon experience.

On another occasion a constituent, a personal friend, had come to Washington to accompany a top official in his company, who was scheduled to testify before a subcommittee of which I am a member. As it happened, I had three committee meetings at the same time, and had to attend first the one in which votes had been scheduled. When I arrived at the hearing my friend and his boss had gone.

That, too, is a common experience.

And then there are the receptions.

Being in Congress is like living with a whole sorority house full of Jewish mothers, and a new batch every week. Receptions pile on dinners, banquets pile on breakfasts, anchovies pile on buffalo-burgers, and at each party, reception and get-together we are buried under drinks, sandwiches and whatever exotic dish is being pushed that night by the Honey Growers, Peanut Growers, Cattle Ranchers, Wheat Growers, Sorghum Industry or Borscht Bottlers Association.)

Every organization in every state apparently feels duty-bound to meet at least once each year with that state's congressional delegation. They meet at breakfasts, lunches, dinners, afternoon receptions, evening receptions.

I've heard members of Congress defend their frequent attendance at lobbyist receptions by claiming that much of the actual business of Congress takes place at these important social gatherings. What takes place is that Congressmen get fat (the Scarsdale diet has been added to the menu in the House dining room), a few get late dates or new phone numbers, and most get totally bored as they check their schedules to see what's next and where.

(One result of all this is that members of Congress are constantly on diets. The House of Representatives lost five tons last year, not by accident, the way the old Department of Health, Education and Welfare lost seven billion dollars, but on purpose. It lost those five tons on starvation diets, grapefruit diets, Scarsdale diets and last-chance diets, and it lost most of it between the first of March and the end of September, the months when members of Congress pose for billboards, campaign brochures and the tube.)

Nor is weight the only problem. Evening receptions take time away from family and work. (Receptions never come singly; they seem to be scheduled in duplicate, triplicate and quadruplicate, three, four or more a night, and each is attended by at least one constituent who cannot understand how one two-hour reception after work is such an inconvenience.)

But I can't really find it in my heart to complain about the noon and night-time receptions and dinners. There are also those who schedule breakfast meetings. Breakfast meetings are, of course, the most convenient. The hosts merely rise, dress, and take an elevator down four floors to the rented meeting room. (For the first three years I was in Congress, I lived 21 miles away from the Capitol, along a route that runs past the Pentagon; attending an 8 a.m. breakfast required leaving the house by 6:15—if I waited until 6:30 and got caught in the early-morning traffic, I would get there just as breakfast ended.)

Of course, House rules do not require that all invitations be accepted, but as a matter of practical politics, if a constituent, or several, will be at the meeting or reception, a Congressman concerned about his re-election will try to appear.

(I admit that I enjoyed some benefit in my first Congressional campaign from the people who came to my meetings and said, "you know, we go to Washington to meet with our Congressman, and old John never shows up." John's failure to show up won me a few votes. I'm sorry, John).

On September 19, 1978, I received invitations to:

An Alaskan King Crab Feed sponsored by the Congressman from Alaska. I said no.

A 2 p.m. ceremony to install the members of the National Advisory Council on Women's Educational Programs. (The bottom of the letterhead listed one woman as "chair" and another as "vice-chair"; I almost attended just to see a woman who was also a chair, but sent my regrets.)

A reception for a lady who had just been appointed vice president of the Educational Testing Service, Washington Office. (If concern with educational programs and educational testing held any promise of improving the quality of education—say the basic ability to read, write, spell, add, multiply, etc., the temptation would have been greater.) Sorry.

An invitation to attend a reception put on by the Eastern European Travel Board, the Soviet airline, the Czech airline, the Polish airline, and the tourist agencies of Bulgaria, East Germany, Cuba, Poland, Czechoslovakia and the Soviet Union, who were going to have an exhibit at the Oklahoma State Fair. I love my state; I love its state fair; I did not go to the reception.

A reception in honor of the 10th anniversary of the Council on Legal Education Opportunity (more education; what a hopeful sign this is). I said no.

A reception in honor of the founding of the Republic of China; a reception in honor of the International Chairman of the "Educate for Peace" Committee of the World Fellowship of Religions; a dinner for the minister of finance of Chile; and a reception and luncheon for the United Fresh Fruit and Vegetable Association. No, no, no, no. Sorry.

A reception to celebrate the publication of a new book by the Institute for the Study of Education Policy (take heart, parents, education is uppermost in our minds); an invitation to attend a Forum for the Arts (featuring Chinese, American and Italian food; Gourmet Alley; the French Onion, and Swensen's Ice Cream. Burp!) No thanks.

A reception in honor of a Puerto Rican pianist; a reception to see the new offices of the Bendix Corporation; a reception to see the new cars being offered by General Motors. Regrets. Regrets. Regrets.

A summer music festival; a state fair; a golf tournament; a Texas "good time" party; a reception for the Northwest Iowa Community Conference, and a reception for the American Paper Institute.

It's hard enough to shed pounds; maybe it would be better if we could shed the receptions.

The result of all this—the backlogged receptions, the constituents who drop by the office several times a day during the tourist season, the three committee meetings at once, the 600 or 700 votes a year—is that there is simply no time for a Congressman to do the job he was elected to do, and that is to think about the issues facing America and what to do about them.

2. Home Is Where the Power Is

Nor are the hundreds of votes and thousands of cumulative receptions, meetings, hearings and other goings-on in Washington the principal thieves in whose knapsacks time for reflection is stolen away.

Nor does the time steal away to the corner malt-shop in the pockets of staff members whose principal means of assistance is to generate more work for the Congressmen they were hired to relieve of work; nor is it spent in finding out why it takes weeks or months to reply to a constituent's letter, or in approving various arrangings and rearrangings of staff and desks in pursuit of an elusive efficiency that perhaps is allergic to Washington in any case.

The fact is, many of those mercury-coated slick-as-a whistle minutes are not in Washington at all.

When one thinks of a Congressman, one usually thinks of a scene in Washington—an image cultivated by Congressmen who distribute pictures of themselves with the Capitol dome in the background (or, if they are trying to impress voters with their youth and vitality, dashing up the Capitol steps).

Washington indeed plays a major role in a Congressman's life and job. But the picture would be more accurate if he were shown standing at the busiest intersection in the congressional district he represents. "The district" dominates the Congressman's life and decisions. What the editors of the *Washington Post* think about an issue is not nearly so important as an editorial, column or letter in the smallest weekly back home. A letter from the President is not as persuasive as a letter from the President of a local Chamber of Commerce or a dozen angry ladies who drafted a letter at a meeting of their bridge club or the local BPW. It's simply a matter of remembering which people can vote for you (or against you) and which cannot.

It would also be more accurate to picture a Congressman back home because that's where he spends a good part of his time. During my first term in office, for example, I spent nearly 250 days in Oklahoma. I spent almost every weekend there. I spent almost every day of every recess—whether the House was out of session for week or a month—in Oklahoma. Other Congressmen may not spend as much time in their home districts as I do, but most of them spend a lot of time there. I don't know any who fail to go back several days a month, and many are virtually commuters.

Washington is an oasis of exercised brain-waves, an oak-lined, thought-filled library compared with the moving sidewalks back home. Breakfast meetings, lunch meetings, dinner meetings—sometimes 150 miles apart; constituent meetings stacked 15 minutes apart from nine in the morning until half-past seven.

Typical days in the district always begin the same way—with a phone call. I have been awakened by constituents calling as early as 5 a.m., and on those rare mornings when there is no morning meeting I rarely get past 7 a.m. without the first call. (If I'm particularly tired, having returned, perhaps, from the far reaches of the district sometime between 1 and 2 in the morning, I simply unplug the phone. I am tempted to do that more often than I do).

It is not out of nobility that I leave the telephone (one of mankind's two most abysmal inventions) in working condition; it is simply that most calls are not from kooks or cranks but instead from people who need help in a hurry. (Sometimes it is a matter a constituent trying to get a federal disability check he is entitled to because he is down to his last few dollars and in danger of losing his home—something that happens far more often than it should because federal agencies are frequently both incompetent and uncaring in processing claims.) In defining what's urgent and what's not, one has to remember how meaningless something may be to the community at large and how transcendent in the life of the individual who is calling. When handling a constituent problem, a Congressman isn't dealing with issues of war and peace, he is dealing with problems in life, and issues that may seem minor at the State Department are of great concern to the person who calls. The average American has never called his or her Congressman, or written to him. It takes a major problem to move somebody to take that step, and I try to keep that in mind with each call.

Early in my first term in office, I received a call from a lady whose daughter had taken part in a protest demonstration against the Seabrook Nuclear Facility in New Hampshire. Governor Meldrim Thompson had responded by breaking up the rally and locking the protestors into a large gymnasium. The mother was worried because she knew her daughter had no money, could not put up bail, and faced a long weekend in the Governor's makeshift jail.

I had long advocated the development of nuclear power as an energy alternative (although I have since become increasingly concerned about some of the inadequacies in the way both utilities and the government meet their responsibilities), but at that point my attention was not on nuclear power but on the rights of my constituent—or anybody else's—to demonstrate peacefully. At that time my views were diametrically opposite those of the constituent's daughter, but she was entitled to be able to protest. If she was guilty of anything—such as trespass—there were proper penalties, it seemed, short of her summary imprisonment.

I phoned the armory where she was being held and asked to speak to her. A police sergeant told me she would not be allowed to come to the phone. I was outraged then, and am still, that a teenage girl being held in detention for the act of protesting against a state energy policy (and for not having money for bail) would be denied the right to talk to her Congressman if *he* called *her*. Furious, I called the governor's office. On my next call to the armory, the girl was permitted to come to the phone. (As is happened, there appeared to be little I could do to get the girl out of the armory, and neither she nor her mother had the money to put up bail. I wired the bail money to her myself. I've never heard from her since; not so much as a thank-you, and have never been repaid. But I would do it again.)

I have called military commanders at their bases in Europe on Sunday afternoons; I have tracked down state social workers in the middle of the night; I have walked in unannounced on the heads of government agency offices in Oklahoma City and forced them to answer questions for constituents who accompanied me.

That has become an important part of the job. And it, too, like the weekend town meetings, the countless hours at countless coffees, takes away the time for reflection on the issues we will be called upon to settle when we return to Washington.

The time at home is important—the essence of American politics. If a representative's job is to represent, it is the time in the Oklahomas and Montanas and New Jerseys that must shape what the Congress does. But there is a tradeoff. As we learn more about what our constituents want us to do—thanks to the telephones, air travel and sophisticated polling techniques—we have less time to do it right.

A Congressman's job has expanded to include roles as ombudsman, social worker, professional lunch-goer and speech-giver. It is not that these roles are improperly part of a Congressman's job description; it is simply that as demands expand and time does not, the minutes spent on deliberative thought are fewer in each session of the Congress and the results predictably worse.

3. Frustration and Filters: Dealing with the Press

There is yet another frustration that plagues members of Congress—and almost everybody else in public life.

In the "Miss Peach" comic strip, the editor of the "Kelly School Klarion" asks, "Arthur, what's the headline on that story about Mister Grimmis losing his wallet, complete with driver's license, I.D., and everything?"

He replies, "Principal of Kelly School Found Lacking Credentials".

We know how Mr. Grimmis feels.

Before I was elected to Congress I was, among other things, an attorney, though I never practiced law much and had no real desire to do so. Nonetheless, I had remained a member of the Oklahoma Bar Association, which entitled me to represent friends if they insisted, and to read the monthly Bar Journal, participate in a group insurance program and receive other assorted benefits.

While my annual dues of $100 a year may have helped the Association meet its expenses, I soon concluded that being a Congressman left precious little time to practice law if I wanted to, and no time to read the magazine. So when the bill arrived for my membership dues, I tossed it in the wastebasket; and the one after that. Eventually I received a letter explaining that if I didn't pay my dues I would no longer be a member, which sounded reasonable enough, just as I was not a member of any other organization I chose not to join. So when the time came for the periodic purging of the mailing lists, my name was removed.

One night I received a phone call at home from a reporter for a newspaper in the district. He had seen the Bar Association's list of persons dropped from its rolls and wanted to know why my name was on it. Simple, I said; I had chosen not to renew my membership.

The next day the newspaper printed the names of persons who were no longer members of the Oklahoma Bar Association. The headline:

Edwards
Suspended
By Bar

Such relationships with the press make the life of any public figure less tranquil.

Reporters, it seems, are frequently concerned with things different than the things their subjects (or their readers) are concerned with. At one point, while I was deeply involved in the national debate over ratification of the proposed Panama Canal treaties—an issue that dominated political discussion in my home district—a reporter for an Oklahoma City newspaper told me he had no interest whatsoever in the Panama Canal debate or my role in it; his sole interest, he said, was in knowing when Oklahoma City was due to receive some sort of federal grant, or additional money for one of its myriad lake, highway or community development projects.

Perspectives, obviously, are different.

Suspicion is a necessary ingredient of a reporter's job; the reporter who unfairly assigns wrongful motives to a subject he is covering does a disservice to that subject but a reporter who gullibly accepts whatever somebody on the public payroll tells him may be doing a disservice to the whole society.

Nonetheless I sometimes wonder if it's not possible for such relationships to be improved.

In 1980 I spoke to a meeting of the state executive committee of the Oklahoma Republican Party. Ed Montgomery, then the political reporter for the *Daily Oklahoman*, wrote:

"Congressman Mickey Edwards took his fellow state Republican leaders to task Saturday for not broadening their base by appealing to a wider range of voters."

After I returned to Washington, the chief of the newspaper's Washington bureau, Allan Cromley, asked me about the speech. I reminded him that I had been saying the same thing for a long time. I also pointed out that my idea of a "conservative" viewpoint might not be what *he* considered to be the "conservative" view.

Cromley's column on the editorial page of the following Sunday's newspaper analyzed my "move to the left". As one example he used my speech to Republicans in Oklahoma City the previous week. Yet Cromley, himself, in a column written two years earlier, in April of 1978, had written:

Edwards is also sharply critical of conservatives who merely criticize the initiatives of the liberals. When Democrats introduced the Humphrey-Hawkins bill to decrease employment, "we conservatives didn't even acknowledge there was unemployment," he said.

"We've got to get specific. We can't just go around with cliches and one-liners."

"In a long memorandum on proposed action for the conservative movement," Edwards said, "if a black cannot rise above poverty because an employer discriminates against him, a recital of the employer's right to discriminate is both constitutionally and philosophically correct and wholly inadequate as a political response..."

"Opposition to wrong solutions is not a political program."

Two years before, on December 4, 1976, Ed Montgomery, the reporter in Oklahoma City, had attended a press conference I held soon after my election. The headline: "Edwards Sees Broader Party Approach." The article reported my comments urging the Republican Party to expand its concerns to address the aspirations of minorities and blue collar workers.

Now, four years later, an article on the editorial page of the largest newspaper in my district was talking about my "move to the left," oblivious to what the same reporter, and another, had written in the same newspaper off and on for a period of nearly four years.

The result of such reporting is an enormous frustration that causes people in public life to rely on newsletters, direct mail and television and radio interviews to get around the press filters that stand in the way of giving the public a clear picture of what they are all about.

At one point, after a similar incident, I stood in the Speaker's Lobby, just off the House floor, talking with Vivian Vahlberg, another reporter for the *Oklahoman* (and later the first woman to become president of the National Press Club).

"You've got to understand," she said, "that there's an ebb and flow in your relationship with the press, just as there is in all other relationships."

And she's right. But an "ebb" in the relationship between a political figure and the reporters who determine what the public will see of him can damage or destroy a career in public life. It is different enough from other relationships that the press, if it is to regain the public's confidence, must begin to impose upon itself the internal checks and restraints that will permit it to do its job as the watchdog for society without injecting itself into the political process either by failing to report or by reporting unfairly. A free press—unrestrained by law or force—is essential to a free society. If public confidence in the objectivity of the press is diminished, the damage to individual persons or careers will be far less than the damage to society as a whole.

4. All or Nothing: The Politics of Confrontation

There is yet another great source of frustration in the Congress. There are no grays.

Politics seems inevitably to lead to confrontations where none need exist, to fixed and inflexible positions where compromise would better serve. Amazingly, to the casual observer outside the Congress, the opposite seems true. To many, "compromise" and "politics" are terms which are virtually interchangeable.

At one level of the process that is certainly true; supporters of a proposition may indeed soften their original positions (or strengthen them) in order to win support they might not otherwise have had. This most frequently happens in the initial stages of consideration, when a bill is being drafted originally, or when it is first brought to a subcommittee for consideration.

In rare instances, as was the case in the protracted debate over the Alaskan Lands Bill, pressure from Alaskans, including a threatened filibuster in the Senate, led eventually to a diluted bill that was more acceptable, both in the Congress and in Juneau.

After that initial stage, however,—and it frequently does not take place at all—sides are formed and proceed to contest the shape of proposed legislation. In many cases there are two sides—conservative or liberal, big government or small, more regulation or less. In the Interior Committee there are often three sides—a "liberal" pro-environmental position, presented by committee chairman Mo Udall, usually including some concessions to make the legislation more palatable; an even more liberal position, representing the outer extremes of the environmental movement, usually led by John Seiberling, of Ohio, and the conservative, or Republican position, which will vary from total opposition to an attempt to pass amendments (to allow more exploration and production of potential energy reserves, for example).

While what finally emerges from the committee will often be a mixture of the various viewpoints, that is not the result of compromise, as it is usually conceived, but of a clash of ideas in which no side wins everything it wanted. The end result, so far as the legislation is concerned, may be almost the same as if there had been compromise originally. But the end result so far as the individual member is concerned is quite different, for while the confrontation method may ultimately produce the same results, it forces each member to vote yes or no, up or down, one way or the other, on a whole series of questions on which he or she may honestly feel that the proper answer is somewhere in the middle.

Let me offer an example: Assume that a bill before the committee provides that the entire state of North Nowhere is to be set aside in various forms of protection—wilderness areas, refuges, parks, scenic rivers, and so forth—and nowhere in the state is the land to be despoiled by such activities as drilling, mining, damming, felling timber, or the like.

You, on the other hand, believe the proper position is somewhere in between; North Nowhere is a beautiful place, and you want it to be preserved not only for the pleasure of backpackers, but also for the pleasure, ultimately, of your own grandchildren. At the same time, however, the United States is in the midst of an energy crisis, with the country increasingly dependent on unreliable (and expensive) foreign sources.

The Sierra Club, Friends of the Earth, and other environmental groups protest any plans to interfere with what God has so well situated on North Nowhere's surface. Production-minded people, including those who would ultimately be paid to do the mining, drilling, etc., object to legislation that would make forever unavailable the abundant life-enhancing (and maybe even life-preserving) resources God has so well situated just beneath the ground throughout large parts of the state.

You may, of course, offer your own solution as an amendment: Let's lock up, say, 80 percent of the state, forever protected from those boors and clods who litter the ground with beer cans and weiner wrappers;

let's pick out another 20 percent of the state, that part which research indicates has the best potential for yielding energy supplies, and allow energy production to go on there, so we'll have fuel to heat our homes and factories, and so more of North Nowhere's citizens will have jobs.

Despite your efforts, however, your amendment is defeated.

This, is what then happens—and it is, in fact, precisely what happens, eventually, in every legislative battle on the floor or in committee: There is finally a vote on the bill, take it or leave it, in whatever shape it's now in. If you vote *against* it, you are identifying yourself to your colleagues, your constituents and your grandchildren as being opposed to environmental protection. You are assigning to yourself a role as protector of the multinational corporations which plan to exploit the land. You are in league with the despoilers of natural beauty. And the various environmental groups will make sure their supporters in your congressional district know of your position. They will (if you regularly come down on that side in such confrontations) rate you as a "zero" on environmental concerns, and will list you as one of the "Dirty Dozen" they have targeted for defeat in the next election.

If you, instead, vote *for* the bill, you are identifying yourself to the same people as someone totally oblivious to the great energy crisis within the country. Business groups which are increasingly concerned about the availability of energy supplies will rate you as mercilessly as would the environmentalists, and even if you can find this position easier to live with politically (because many businessmen—especially the managers of large corporations—do not have the courage of their convictions and tend to support incumbents anyway, regardless of what they believe or how they vote), it is nonetheless true that you will still have to live with yourself and the fact that you have signaled to your friends and society at large a position that is not really what you believe at all.

The example is a totally accurate portrayal of the position in which we find ourselves almost every day. When it comes to final passage on any bill or resolution before the House, there are only three choices: yes, no, or "present". One cannot vote, "yes, if..." or "no, but..." And we are all therefore judged by decisions made in response to Hobson's Choices that may in no way truly reflect "who we are" or "where we're coming from," and that knowledge, and the desire to have people see you as you really are, can exert a powerful psychological pull.

It is one reason why I have chosen to write this book.

CHAPTER SEVEN
NEW DIRECTIONS

1. Building a Bridge to Black America

During the 95th Congress, the Republican Party began to take its first tentative steps toward a rapprochement with black Americans—a reconciliation that will remain difficult for some time to come, but which must take place if the Republican Party is ever to regain long-term preeminence in American politics.

Getting blacks and Republicans back together will not be an easy matter. Just how difficult the job will be was spelled out by Wendell Gunn, a black banker, in an article in the *Lincoln Review*.

> Yes, black America is dissatisified with the Democrats. But we have a long history of dissatisfaction with the Republicans. If the Republican Party is going to attract black Americans in large numbers into its ranks, I can tell you now that depending on black dissatisfaction with Democrats will be no more effective than relying on the residual effects of Lincoln's Emancipation Proclamation. Republicans will have to do something positive in order to dispel the negative reputation they have earned among blacks.

And *that* comes from a black who writes such things as, "The only thing that can release black America from its apparent dependence on income redistribution is real private sector economic expansion." If *he* says blacks are not ready yet to end their long alliance with the Democrats, what can Republicans hope for?

In 1976 black voters played a major role in Jimmy Carter's election strategy. Although it doesn't make them at all unique, a lot of those blacks who voted for Carter soon began to wish they hadn't.

Why did they vote for Carter in the first place? And in such overwhelming numbers: Gerald Ford admittedly didn't inspire great enthusiasms, but neither had he done anything to alienate blacks. He slept on his sheets; he didn't wear them.

What he had done wrong, mostly, was to be a Republican. And since the decision to vote against him turned out so badly, some black voters began contemplating just where it gets them to vote more or less automatically for whomever the Democrats put up.

There is, in fact, an increasing awareness among black politicians that their traditional allies, the Democrats, have begun to take them for granted. No more posies and presents.

And there has been an increasing awareness among Republicans, at the same time, that unless they somehow get some more votes, somewhere, on a more or less regular basis, the Grand Old Party won't be at the party any more. (A Ronald Reagan, unique in his charisma, and a Jimmy Carter, unique in his nearly total lack of it, can, when coupled with inflation, Iranian hostages, and a beginning recession, produce Republican victories. But the Republican Party, as a party, was the beneficiary, not the star, of the 1980 elections.)

Wendell Gunn wrote: "Now that we are not legally prohibited from participating in the economy, the economy must be allowed to expand in order for our struggle to have been truly worthwhile."

Gunn sees this central need of blacks as the Republican opportunity to "dispel the negative reputation" the GOP has built among blacks for many years.

High taxes, high inflation rates and high interest rates—the products of liberal spending policies—tend to restrict economic growth, and for blacks those policies are bad news indeed. So long as blacks are getting the smallest piece of the pie, the only way they're going to get a good slice is to have a bigger pie.

(A similar thought once prompted a number of blacks within the NAACP to stray temporarily off the liberal reservation and call for the deregulation of natural gas prices: unless more energy is produced, they reasoned, there will be fewer new jobs created; unless more new jobs are created, blacks will continue to be plagued by high rates of unemployment. They later retreated from the farthest reaches of that new philosophical frontier, but the venture sent shock waves rippling through an already-reeling liberal community.)

Nor is this the only example of a blossoming black discontent with traditional liberal programs and solutions.

Professor Thomas Sowell, who is black, claimed in an article in the *New York Times Sunday Magazine* that for white liberals championing the cause of disadvantaged blacks had become a choice occupation. "To be blunt," he said, "the poor are a gold mine." Programs to help poor blacks, Sowell said, have helped many a white liberal become rather well off with government funds.

Another black professor, Walter Williams, has accused a traditional black ally, organized labor, of racism: "Organized labor, with but few exceptions," he claims, "has sought to exclude Negroes and other minorities from many job markets. . ."

Williams claims that labor union support for an ever-higher minimum wage "discriminates against low skilled workers." As a result, he says, "it will have its greatest adverse impact on youth in general and minority youth in particular."

It is against this background that the Republican Party is attempting somewhat awkwardly to build a bridge to a segment of the population it has pretty well ignored for many years now.

In 1978, Senate Republican Leader Howard Baker and House Republican Leader John Rhodes put together a task force of senators and Congressmen to try to bridge the gap. The task force met for a few minutes one noon with a handful of Republican-oriented blacks from various parts of the country, and then faded into oblivion. Other efforts have been started and have sputtered to similar conclusions.

There have been attempts to "send signals"—once by getting Jesse Jackson to speak to the Republican National Committee—but blacks remain uncertain what message the signals were meant to convey.

Liberal policies and programs are destroying growth and opportunity. If not one new job was created in America this year, the haves would continue to have; no member of any country club would miss a meal. But *black* opportunity depends on a growing economy—on lower taxes, less regulation, reduced inflation.

The Republican party, if it is to win a share of the black vote, must address itself to the aspirations and hopes of black Americans. The United States may be a nation that prides itself on its charitable impulse, but its *essence*, that which sets the United states apart from other nations, both historically and in the contemporary world, is opportunity.

The cry coming from black Americans is a cry for a chance to make it in the system. And *that* is the cry Republicans must respond to if their fishing expedition is to bring up more than rubber tires and old shoes.

During the Congressional debate on a proposed minimum wage increase, I met in Oklahoma City with Jim Wallace, the director of the OIC program in Oklahoma. (OIC trains unemployed young people for productive work by equipping them with basic job skills; like Wallace, most of the enrollees in the program are black.) Wallace—and his "students"—urged that the minimum wage increase be defeated.

A short time earlier, President Carter's Labor Secretary, Ray Marshall, had testified before the House Education and Labor Committee. In his testimony, Marshall conceded that the increased wage requirement would probably result in a loss of jobs—some 90,000 by his estimate. Marshall, of course, considered the number of lost jobs to be relatively small and a worthwhile sacrifice to achieve a greater good.

Jim Wallace clearly understood what this typical well-meaning liberal initiative would mean to unemployed blacks, and to those employed blacks at the bottom of the ladder who would be the first to be fired. But the case was best put by one of the young blacks enrolled in the OIC program:

"It may not be very many jobs that will be lost," he said—"but they're *our* jobs."

Ben Tipton, a black Democrat who once served as a member of the city council in Oklahoma City, came to my office one morning. He had been injured in an automobile accident a few days earlier; he left the hospital to meet with me, his face swollen and bandaged.

"Mickey," he said. "We need your help to break out of this welfare cycle and start on a work cycle."

He outlined the same story I had been hearing from hundreds of Oklahoma blacks, at neighborhood meetings, at Urban League dinners, at churches, at Soul Bazaars, from the blacks on my Congressional staff—in fact, from almost every black I talked to (except for the members of the Congressional Black Caucus, who ostensibly speak in the Congress for blacks, but seldom seem to hear what the blacks I know are saying.)

Blacks and whites are not intrinsically different, and it is insulting and inaccurate to suggest that they are. Why do liberal politicians believe that whites want two cars, a nice home in the suburbs, college education and careers, but blacks want bigger welfare checks, lowered educational standards and weekly visits by social workers?

When standards are lowered for blacks, it is blacks who suffer. What blacks want is federally-enforced removal of artificial barriers to their progress and, where necessary, some assistance from the community to clear those barriers that have already decreased their chances of competing successfully in the marketplace.

Many liberals have been surprised by black support for such conservative Republican initiatives as school voucher systems and tuition tax credits for private education.

In his book, *Black Education: Myths and Tragedies*, Thomas Sowell spells out the problem: "Many of the problems of black students in college," he says, "can be traced to inadequate education preparation in the public schools."

The solution? Sowell suggests a voucher system under which parents could enroll their children either in public school or wherever else they may choose.

"The violent controversy surrounding the idea is due to the devastating impact it could have on vested interests in the present institutional structure of the American public schools...voucher systems are no panacea. All that can be claimed for them is that they offer important benefits not obtainable under the existing institutional structure, without making the other problems any worse. In the world as it is, that is a very large advantage."

Another prominent black, Roy Innis, as national director of the Congress of Racial Equality, expressed similar concern about the public school barrier to black advancement, and offered another solution straight out of the Republican platform:

"It is rather curious, that CORE's support for the passage of the tuition tax credit Bill should at the same time surprise so many of our traditional 'conservative' opponents and offend so many of our traditional 'liberal' allies. Nonetheless, it is my judgement that the root of this reaction is the belief that the education of blacks (especially elementary and secondary education) should somehow remain synonymous with public education. In other words blacks, especially

low to moderate income blacks, should not be afforded the same opportunity to exercise the kind of educational options enjoyed by the
more fortunate members of American society.''

These clearly are not the words that politicians are used to hearing
from black leaders.

For the most part, the nation's most prominent black politicians do
not represent the true aspirations of most black Americans. (That, of
course, is not an unusual phenomenon; as the George Wallace campaigns proved, national labor leaders often did not represent the views
of those whose dues paid their salaries.)

Because so few blacks have been elected to public office, those who
are elected achieve a great prominence within the black community
and assume the responsibility of speaking for ''blacks.'' (Of course, the
obvious question is, if the Congressional Black Caucus doesn't speak
for blacks, who does? White Republicans? Of course not: the answer is,
nobody speaks for blacks, any more than Bella Abzug can claim to
speak for women, or Jimmy Carter—or Ronald Reagan—for whites or
men.)

While members of the Congressional Black Caucus are highly in-
telligent, articulate, deeply motivated and competent members of
Congress, they represent not all blacks but the unique urban constitu-
encies which elected them, and, in addition, they represent their own
political philosophies. I speak for the views I hold, and the views of my
constituents; I do not speak for ''whites.'' It is no different with Ron
Dellums or Parren Mitchell. They are Democrats and liberals; they
speak from a liberal perspective.

Clearly black politicians who put their liberalism ahead of their
blackness are doing only what other politicians do. I put my beliefs
and principles ahead of my ''whiteness'' (and would be called a racist if
I did not). But the Republican Party must understand that lesson. If
the Republican Party is to win back votes, it cannot do so just by hypo-
critically echoing whatever the members of the Black Caucus propose.
Blacks will not vote for Republicans, *and should not*, until Republicans
show by their own continuing actions and their own search for
opportunity-enhancing solutions, that they truly care not just about
black votes but about black people.

Blacks differ from white voters in this respect: Whereas white
voters may list as their first concern the inflation rate (or taxes, or the
availability of jobs), blacks will list as their first interest a desire for pol-

iticians who care about people—*after which* they will follow with the same checklist of problems and concerns shared by non-blacks.

Arthur J. Finkelstein & Associates, a leading New York-based political survey firm, completed attitudinal surveys of Oklahoma's Fifth Congressional District in July, 1976; September, 1976; February, 1978; and July, 1978. Some of what Finkelstein found reinforced my own awareness that liberal blacks in Congress do not speak for the blacks I represent (by a two-to-one margin, for example, blacks in my completely urban district opposed forced busing for purposes of school integration, and by a similar margin they opposed federal funding of abortions, yet both busing and abortion are supported in Congress by the Black Caucus, supposedly in the name of black voters).

But the most significant finding of the surveys was this:

Asked what their greatest concerns were, voters in every section of the district gave nearly identical answers (inflation, etc.) *except* in the area which is predominantly black. There the principal response was a search for somebody who is "for the people."

No political essay can say it as eloquently. Blacks have problems that whites—or at least, most whites—don't have. It is only recently that members of their families have gone to college or received a decent high school education. Colleges with open admissions policies and sympathetic administrations and faculties still cannot make up for the lack of basic skills. Blacks who want to go out into business for themselves find that they are considered such high-risk investments that it is difficult for them to get adequate initial financing (often loans are limited to amounts that doom the whole project in advance—enough money to open the doors and stock the shelves, but not enough for operating capital until the business can begin to show a profit; the result is debt and bankruptcy and a bitter would-be black businessman worse off than he was before).

Republican efforts to attract black votes (and ensure Republican survival) simply won't work unless the GOP grasps the basic fact that the name of the game is, simply, opportunity. In Walter Williams' words: "Black people, like poor minorities of the past, do not need federal handouts and gifts. Black people need a chance to compete."

Wendell Gunn is right: Republicans must do something *positive* if they are to compete for the black vote—and what they must do is address themselves to the central problem of black existence: the inability to get into the system.

So long as Republicans attempt to get black votes with superficial rhetoric, blacks will continue to cast most of their votes for Democrats—out of habit, if nothing else.

During the 1978 elections, two leading white political figures in Oklahoma, one a Republican and one a Democrat, asked Russell Perry, a black newspaper publisher, for his support. They said (as had several other lesser political figures) that they wanted "to put together the kind of support Mickey Edwards has" in the black community.

One cannot "put together" black support. If you care about blacks and their problems, black votes will follow. Attempt to fool blacks by copying Democrats, and blacks, forced to choose between real Democrats and phony Democrats will, naturally, vote for the real thing, while white conservatives will abandon the Republican Party and it will soon sink, deservedly, into oblivion.

Louisiana Congressman Bob Livingston and Senator Pete Domenici, of New Mexico, once drafted a resolution adopted unanimously by national Republican leaders meeting at the annual, informal, Tidewater Conference. The resolution called for:

• Tax incentives to expand employment opportunities in private industry;

• A redirection of resources within vocational education to address the high rates of unemployment among youth and minorities, and

• Offering appropriate incentives for the voluntary relocation of the labor force to areas where job opportunities may be more plentiful.

There are obviously additional ways in which the GOP can address black problems:

• Re-evaluate SBA loan procedures, which have brought harsh criticism from would-be black businessmen.

• Develop incentives to encourage lenders to make high-risk or "soft" loans.

• Develop incentives to encourage savings programs to generate risk capital within the black community.

• Encourage programs to train potential black entrepreneurs—programs like the private Interracial Council for Business Opportunity in New York City.

There are a number of other possible approaches to developing black businesses, some of which are explored in the book *Black Capitalism: Strategy for Business in the Ghetto,* by Theodore L. Cross, written from his vantage point as chairman of the Banking Law Institute.

Some of these proposals may work; others may not. But it is evident that Republicans can address black needs from within the framework of Republican philosophy. If the Republican Party is to be a national party, it must concern itself with the hopes and aspirations of *all* Americans, black as well as white. It can do so without changing its basic political premise because free enterprise, which the Republican Party holds out as its alternative, is the only way in which black Americans can move a step further, into what Wendell Gunn calls "The Civil Rights Struggle: Phase II."

If the Republican Party does indeed reach an accommodation with black voters, the result could be the most profound long-term change in the direction of American politics since the beginning of Franklin D. Roosevelt's "New Deal."

2. Behind Enemy Lines: Republicans in the Union Hall

For the past 40 years American politics has centered on a continuing conflict between two separate elements of the productive society—the capital producers, who provide the product and create the jobs—and the workers, who transform the capital into finished, useful goods or services.

Confrontation has been the most constant ingredient in the continuing relationship between labor and management in the United States. Time and again, the big guns of labor and industry have been rolled out in massive campaigns that stir animosities, drain resources and divide the nation.

But both labor and management seem to be undergoing a metamorphosis as foreign competition closes in on domestic markets and common interests—and common fears—begin to supersede traditional patterns of hostility and distrust.

The emergence of a potential new consensus struck me full force late one afternoon in a motel room in Youngstown, Ohio.

It was a bitterly cold day in Youngstown, and as chilly inside the room as out. I sat with Illinois Congressman Philip Crane, facing half a dozen suspicious and hostile local labor union leaders. The blast furnaces were idle, people were out of work, the city was in trouble, and we were only marginally welcome there.

That trip—a conservative venture into labor union territory—was, for me, a second trip behind enemy lines (as somebody had put it, if Sadat could fly to Israel, why couldn't Republicans go to union halls?). But our presence in that room could not have seemed stranger to the union members than it had to us when the idea had first been proposed on a winter night, not too long before, in the home of Richard Viguerie, a soft-spoken direct mail specialist who had risen to prominence—and controversy—as a result of his success in raising campaign funds for conservative candidates. We had gathered that night, as we had on several previous occasions, not to discuss a trip to Youngstown, but to plan the presidential campaign of Phil Crane, who was then the national chairman of the American Conservative Union and a leading spokesman for conservative political thought.

We had each come to the Crane campaign—and now to this attempt to bridge the gap between conservatives and labor—in different ways. It had begun for me at a small dinner party a few months before, that one, too, in Viguerie's Virginia home. There were a handful of us present—Viguerie, Crane, Rich Williamson (then Crane's top congressional assistant and now a key figure in the Reagan White House), publisher William Rusher (better known as a conservative spokesman on the television program, "The Advocates"), Paul Weyrich, founder of a committee to train conservative candidates, Howard Phillips, national chairman of a group known as the Conservative Caucus, and myself.

At that point, the Crane campaign was designed only to offer Crane national visibility so he could actually seek the presidential nomination in earnest if Ronald Reagan decided not to run, and to position Crane for a major role, either as Reagan's national campaign chairman or as a possible running mate, if Reagan did run. In any event, Crane was to fold his campaign when Reagan announced.

The scenario soon changed in strange ways. Some in the room held a deep hostility toward Reagan, for one reason or another, and fully intended to push Crane's campaign all the way, in a direct challenge to Reagan. But even that revised plot began to fall apart: Within a few months, Viguerie, who did not feel Reagan was conservative enough, had deserted Crane to support John Connally; Weyrich, another who shared that view had also left Crane; Williamson, Crane's campaign manager, was working for Reagan.

But while the Crane campaign was still in its formative stages, we were actively looking for ways to boost both his candidacy and the emerging conservative movement; it was at one of those winter meetings that we began to explore the possibility of taking Phil's candidacy directly to the people in the labor movement.

The conservative movement has been somewhat arbitrarily divided by political observers into two groups: old line conservatives (meaning, I suppose, people like Barry Goldwater and Strom Thrumond) and the so-called New Right, a phrase devised by columnist Kevin Phillips, who had detected major and fundamental differences between the "conservative" America was used to and those of us who had inherited the same label, but who were in fact both more libertarian and more populist in our beliefs.

Unlike traditional Republicans, who often represented wealth and sometimes came from wealthy background themselves, the so-called New Right was made up primarily of people from far more modest beginnings and thus with closer ties to the concerns of working Americans. (Reporters have since redefined Phillips' "New Right," using it as a catchword to indicate those in the conservative movement who have concentrated on the so-called "social agenda"—opposition to busing, the Equal Rights Amendment, abortion and support for a return to prayer in the public schools. As the term was originally coined, however, the "New Right" primarily referred to a new generation of conservatives far more interested in middle-class America—blue-collar workers, union members, blacks, small businessmen and farmers—than in country clubs or the Fortune 500.)

Our original group was a classic example of the changes in "conservatism." Howie Phillips, a huge, imposing man, who had once headed the Office of Economic Opportunity, came from a family of poor Jewish immigrants. Paul Weyrich was the son of a school custodian in Milwaukee. Crane's father is a physician (and a fairly prominent syndicated columnist), but Phil's grandparents worked in the steel mills of South Chicago. I grew up in the poorer neighborhoods of Chicago and Oklahoma City, the grandson of Polish and Lithuanian Jewish immigrants who had scraped out a living sorting scrap metal and peddling rags and cloth goods from carts in the streets of Cleveland. My own father had been raised in an orphanage, and later helped support his younger brothers and sisters. There were no Henry Cabot Lodges or Ohio Tafts in this group.

To this kind of new Republican conservative it was almost unbelievable that the American working man, the assembly line worker, the carpenter, the coal miner, the common laborer, seemed "off-limits." These were *our* people. As a child, I had grown up wearing caps with AFL-CIO buttons on them. This was, indeed, as Kevin Phillips observed, a *new* Right. In many ways we shared the values of older conservatives—we believed in profit as the best incentive to production and as a creator of jobs; we believed in limited government, a strong national defense, maximum individual freedom, less taxation and less regulation. But it was inconceivable to us that the Crane campaign could be required to write off, as so many Republican candidacies did, the votes of America's blue-collar working people.

"Youngstown," Weyrich said.

"What?"

"Youngstown. Let's go to Youngstown."

Youngstown, Ohio, he said, was a perfect example of what we conservatives had been talking about. It was a labor city, a steel town hit by massive unemployment as a result of plant closings which, he believed, could have been avoided, plant closings which were due, in part at least, to government itself.

And so we went to Youngstown. A short time before, in the 1976 elections, the popular mayor of Youngstown, Jack Hunter, a Republican, had run for Congress and had almost won. Now we called Hunter and asked him to help us set up a meeting with local labor officials.

The meeting took place in an isolated corner room in a Youngstown motel. These were rugged, burly men. The small talk was strained. They circled me cautiously with their eyes, alternately wary and hostile. By every tenet of their political faith, every emotional response they had felt since they had first considered politics, I was the enemy. I was a Republican, a conservative—and I was alone; Crane's plane had been delayed.

I was to learn, to my complete amazement, that while Crane and I were indeed perceived to be the "enemy," it was not because we represented a political philosophy *opposed* to big government, but because to their minds, more concerned with livelihood than with the fine points of politics, we *were* that government. We were members of Congress and while we might profess to disagree with the government, to them it was enough that we were *in* the government.

Later, asked how they would describe themselves politically, they all agreed they were liberals. They had long ago come to think of themselves as liberals, and to consider conservatives the enemy of the working man. But if there was a liberal in that room, I'm Tip O'Neill's great-aunt.

One after another, these union leaders, frustrated, angry men, complained...about government! Had that room been bugged, people listening afterwards to the tapes would have thought they had mistakenly tapped into a meeting of a corporate board of directors.

Speaker after speaker angrily denounced the government they had helped to put in office. Their story was a shocking microcosm of the problems that were besetting the whole country. Government spending—and subsequent government borrowing—they said, had dried up the available capital, and the steel mills, which had employed so much of Youngstown's work force, could not get the money they needed for the extensive—and expensive—modernization that was required to remain competitive: money to reline old blast furnaces, for example. The government was failing to enforce anti-dumping laws which provided for automatic tariffs to be imposed on imported products which were sold in the United States at artificially low prices because of subsidies by foreign governments. The Environmental Protection Agency was burying Youngstown's steel manufacturers under a flood of regulations that drove up production costs. OSHA was driving up production costs. Over and over, they repeated the same message—government had caused the massive unemployment in Youngstown.

(Crane had come in during this time and I have wondered whether, walking in on that discussion, he thought for a moment that Hunter had mistakenly set up a meeting with corporate executives or local Republican leaders.)

When the speakers had finished, each punctuating his remarks with fingers pointed sharply at us, Phil and I looked at each other in amazement. These people, who formed the backbone of the Democratic Party, and who even thought of themselves as liberals, sounded as though they were reading from a Republican convention platform.

I was suddenly struck by the enormity of what we had gotten into— the awesome opportunity to bridge the gap between Republican politics and organized labor—but at the same time I was struck by the stunning realization of what a massive communications gap existed between us, a gap, a distrust, so unbelievably large that we could say the same things at the same time and not hear each other.

Like so many other Republican initiatives, however, this one ended up going nowhere. The forces against us and within us were too strong.

That night, we had a small dinner party and invited some members of the press. But while Phil and I were free to talk about what had happened, the union leaders who had met with us refused to show up and be identified publicly for fear of an angry reaction from national union leaders (when the story surfaced, union leaders in Washington exploded in anger and came down so hard on the people in Youngstown that similar meetings were doomed).

Crane and I went back to Washington and drafted a far-reaching legislative package aimed at preventing future Youngstowns—a bill that included incentives to employers to cut other costs before laying off workers, and establishment of a joint labor-management task force to speed up imposition of anti-dumping tariffs to protect against unfairly subsidized foreign competition.

But the bill was introduced in a Congress dominated by Democrats, liberals and labor unions—precisely the identifications these people in Youngstown chose for themselves—and while our initiative received a great deal of press attention, it slipped quietly beneath the ice of Washington and was never seen again, buried in the deep recesses of Congressional committees and subcommittees. And when Phil and I returned to Youngstown a second time, to unveil the legislation we had drafted in specific response to the suggestions of Youngstown labor union officials, not one of them showed up to attend the press conference, or even to meet with us privately. Although a few phoned to let us know of their support and appreciation, not one would risk being seen with us.

Crane's campaign staff inadvertently had further aggravated the situation by aggressively seizing upon the initiative in Youngstown for a massive publicity effort which served to create fears among the union representatives who had met with us that they were "being used."

An attempt to revive the whole Republican-labor operation came a short time later. Crane's office put together a dinner party in Washington and invited John Rhodes, then the Republican leader in the House, a few other Senators and House members, and a sprinkling of labor union members from around the country. The "union representatives" at the dinner were nice enough, but there wasn't a convert among them. They had been Republicans all along, and while the dinner did not represent a step backwards, it was certainly not a very large step forward either. Had this dinner resulted in another meeting of that group at which strategies to seek common ground between Republicans and organized labor were devised, it might have been more significant, but like so many other Republican initiatives it perished at the moment of its birth. So far as I know, the committee was never heard from again.

Ultimately, if America is to retain its high level of affluence and widespread distribution of that affluence, it must find a way to end the war between business and labor. Business must be more sensitive to the real, human needs of its employees, and labor must be more aware of the need to keep business profitable—or jobs, and thus the need for labor unions, will simply disappear.

Am I optimistic that this "millenium" is going to come to pass?

In fact, I am. To some degree the old hostilities will be reduced as new leaders in both business and labor find themselves threatened less by each other and more by common outside enemies, including economic policies that dry up investment capital, foreign competition, dwindling energy supplies, and other factors which threaten employer and employee alike. Labor and management are not opposite sides of the coin. They are the same side—the productive side—and foreign competition and Washington threaten both.

As business and labor improve their perceptions of how the modern world works, as labor's political power continues to fade (requiring it to adapt to a new political balance), as old-style politicians, labor leaders and corporate executives, trained in confrontation, disappear, the gap will be narrowed and the likelihood of common effort increased.

3. The Outsiders: Protectionism and Fortress America

Perhaps the single most important catalytic ingredient in such a massive political realignment will be the increasingly pronounced effect of foreign competition.

In fact, this newly perceived threat to American affluence — this *outside* threat — is part of a much broader picture of change affecting a myriad of relationships internally between Americans and externally between Americans and "outsiders."

There are major political currents swirling under the surface in the United States — currents much like the molten subsurface on which the continental plates float; currents which carry the same potential for friction and social and economic upheaval.

• The United States, economically, is retreating from a free trade bias toward a defensive protectionism which may come increasingly to include sanctions, boycotts and tariffs.

• The American people, until the seizure of the American embassy in Iran and the Soviet invasion of Afghanistan, were retreating perceptibly into an isolationist shell—a movement that has not yet run its course and which threatens to undermine public support for American involvement internationally.

• The United States, culturally and socially, even before the shift of events in Iran, was retreating toward a defensive hostility toward "foreigners"—an almost amazing attitude considering that we are almost all the direct descendants of foreigners ourselves.

The consequences of such changes are almost beyond comprehension. As a result of these three interrelated but distinct tendencies, the America of tomorrow could be greatly different, politically, socially and economically from the America we have known for the past 35 years.

Obviously, foreign-made products, which have become increasingly a part of our lives, would become less present (I am talking not only of steel tubing and pipe, which most Americans never see, but of Panasonic, Sony, Honda, Datsun, Volvo, Volkswagen, Seiko, Leica). But far more important would be the new attitudes of an isolationist America.

There is increasing discussion in the Congress of the need to "protect" a variety of American industries from foreign competition. Members of Congress from the Gulf Coast have introduced and lobbied for legislation to restrict Cuban sugar imports to protect the domestic sugar industry. In 1978, when the House considered appropriations to help finance the World Bank and the International Development Association, an affiliate of the World Bank, it also took up amendments to restrict the lending authority of those two agencies to prevent the use of U.S. funds to subsidize indirectly foreign products in competition with American industry and agriculture.

Whether specific amendments and resolutions succeed or fail is beside the point. In some cases they are not even a fair test of protectionist sentiment (for example, the so-called Cargo Preference Bill, promoted by the maritime unions to protect the American shipping industry, was primarily intended to strengthen union control over the docks). What does matter is the growing frequency with which the Congress discusses efforts to do something about increasingly effective foreign competition.

Clearly it does not matter whether the fault is unfair competition (slave labor, government subsidy, tax preferences) or our own failings (better anticipation by foreign companies of market demands in the United States—the small economy car is a good example—or our own high labor costs).

What *does* matter is (a) that the United States is being increasingly affected by the successes of foreign competitors in their attempts to capture American domestic markets, and (b) a national reaction against foreign competition. This reaction has no geographic or demographic boundaries, nor is it confined philosophically (at least in terms of the usual "conservative" or "liberal" delineations). The reaction affects farmers and their representatives; steel workers and theirs.

It is not an issue without complications. American agricultural and industrial producers need more foreign markets, yet American restrictions on imports will result in a reciprocal closing of our overseas trade markets. The grain farmer doesn't want to endanger his overseas grain markets, but the cattle rancher doesn't want foreign beef imports—and in some instances the same farmer is producing both grain and beef. Oil and gas producers do not want to restrict the availability of foreign drilling pipe (a major pipe shortage disrupted the industry in 1974), but they do want an energy policy that encourages domestic energy production and reduces imports of foreign oil. To some extent it is a case of wanting to have one's cake (restricted imports) and eat it, too (more foreign markets).

Yet one thing is abundantly clear: some foreign governments are pursuing economic policies (wise ones from their point of view) that pose serious threats to the American industrial economy. For example, the Japanese government subsidizes its steel industry in many ways, direct and indirect. On the other hand, the American steel industry has fallen onto hard times, partly as a result of excessive regulations and the massive federal deficit which forced the government to borrow heavily, making money unavailable for plant modernization and expansion.

The Japanese produce high-quality steel for less than we can, and sell it for less, undercutting American producers even in this country's domestic marketplace. American trade law provides for the imposition of special tariffs when foreign countries "dump" products—sell them for artificially low prices—but the tariffs are rarely and slowly imposed. One result: When I introduced the Jobs Stability Act after my 1978 meeting with union leaders in Youngstown, it included creation of a special labor-management team to speed up the placement of tariffs as protection for the domestic steel industry. This was a violation of the principles of international free trade in which I believe; yet without such actions American workers would be out of work in increasing numbers. If breadless people cannot eat cake, neither can jobless

American workers eat free trade philosophy.

When I speak of free trade, I speak of what is today known as free trade. Free trade would literally be unfettered open competition, which means American employers would pay wages based on productivity; American employers would not be handicapped by environmental and job-safety restrictions which go beyond common sense; the government would not soak up the funds needed for modernizing steel plants. As it is, there is no real free trade today, because American manufacturers often must compete at a disadvantage.

The declining United States position in international trade is especially significant in terms of the American presence in Asia. The American economy continues to suffer from a massive national debt and balance-of-payments deficits (resulting from an imbalance in international trade). The Japanese, meanwhile, continue to seek out economic alliances in their best interests. American business—and military planners—must bear these economic realities in mind.

What if, for example, while the Japanese continue their economic expansion, the United States were to pursue the kind of military withdrawal from the Far East that President Carter advocated? Carter toyed with the idea of withdrawing American troops from South Korea (it was General John Singlaub's alarm at this decision that led to his removal as commander of U.S. forces there). President Carter also clearly signaled his intention to turn away further from continued American support of Taiwan, first by pointedly sending Zbigniew Brezinski to Peking on the day Taiwan inaugurated its new President in 1978 (and by sending no official United States representative to Taipei for the inauguration), and later by announcing his decision to stop future sales of American fighter planes to the Taiwan defense forces and to terminate the 1954 mutual defense treaty between Taiwan and the U.S. President Reagan, too, has signaled a reduced American commitment to Taipei.

Early in 1977, as I watched this pattern developing, I began to warn publicly that the United States was creating a serious vacuum in Asia that might force the Japanese to cast about for new Asian allies. Obviously, North Korea and a unified Vietnam are tempting potential markets, with their huge populations and emerging economies. So, too, is the Chinese mainland.

A little over a year later, in the middle of 1978, Japan and China announced the signing of a new friendship agreement, the possible precursor of a major realignment of Asian alliances.

Clearly, not every potential result of America's retrenchment is as dramatic as the shuffle to fill the vacuum in Asia, but there is no question that a national retreat from the world would bring about major changes on many fronts.

It is possible, of course, that the widespread reassessment of America's role in the world following the Russian invasion of Afghanistan will stop this retreat from a major worldwide role, but it is equally likely that the great concerns expressed about diminishing U.S. strength and prestige will ease as the fall of Kabul fades into history and the Soviet Union enters its usual post-invasion period of consolidation—a period that invariably lulls ever-hopeful American liberals back to a complacent sleep. And if that happens, America will continue to diminish not only militarily but also as a force in the world marketplace.

As Americans begin to clamor more loudly for protection from foreign imports which threaten their jobs, as lobbyists seek more boycotts and tariffs, in short, as America becomes more protectionist, we can expect reduced selections of goods and higher prices (imports are almost always cheaper, or they wouldn't be imported). It is a trade-off more and more Americans are apparently willing to make to protect domestic industry and agriculture.

The "Fortress America" syndrome is another matter altogether. It may be alright for Switzerland to become a fortress; nobody is threatening to hammer at the walls. Can an international power suddenly retreat behind its own borders? I doubt it. And there is by no means a consensus to do so. As a national policy, America continues to be determined to involve itself in many ways in world affairs and even in the internal affairs of other nations. President Carter convened a meeting at Camp David with Israeli Prime Minister Menachem Begin and Egyptian Premier Anwar Sadat. President Reagan proposed new partnerships with Canada and Mexico and reaches out to Saudi Arabia and Jordan. Resolutions and letters, which I joined in signing, are sent to the Soviets, protesting the suppression of dissent, in violation of the Helsinki agreements. And increased Cuban and Russian intervention in Africa, rich with mineral resources and vital to the control of the sea lanes, requires at the very least an intense American watchfulness.

But policy decisions at the White House and in the State Department are irrelevant in measuring the national direction. American government responds eventually to the currents in the country, but the signals from the electorate are usually not translated into policy shifts in Washington for a number of years. The instant Congressional reaction to the Jarvis amendment (Proposition 13), which mandated a sharp cut in property taxes in California, came about because the passage of Proposition 13 was not an isolated incident but only the latest and most dramatic in a series of events that included voter rejections of school bonds, library bonds, road bonds, new taxes—almost anything the voters could get their hands on to voice a protest. And only after many of the nation's leading intellectuals had begun to warn more and more often of the dangers in runaway government spending, the growth of government, the waste and ineffectiveness resulting from government programs.

The nation shifts direction before its leaders do—but eventually those "leaders", too, change as they respond to voter pressures or retire (or *are* retired).

Had you taken a public opinion poll before the seizure of our embassy in Iran and the Russian invasion on Afghanistan, you would have found that, except for an occasional mention of concern about the deterioration of the national military strength, virtually nobody at all was giving much thought to what was happening in Africa, Asia or Europe. The conflict between Ethiopia and Somalia, vitally important because of their proximity to the base of the Suez Canal, had stirred virtually no interest. Perhaps that is the way it has always been; certainly the majority of Americans has never been deeply interested in the intricacies of international developments. Since Vietnam, however, the desire to keep the world at arm's length has clearly intensified. Conversations over the past several years with my own constituents, as well with thousands of Americans who have been in my audiences across the country, confirm that we have been developing into a nation with an aversion to foreign involvement, whether that means American troops or something far less. The attitude simply is: That's their business; let's mind our own business. The post-Iran renewal of enthusiasm for foreign affairs will fade unless the Soviet Union alters its historic patterns and makes major new aggressive moves. While Canada, Japan and other countries joined us in responding to the crises in Afghanistan and Iran, the large number of American allies which did not stand with us can only serve to make Americans even less willing to care much about what happens to France, say, or Italy or Mexico.

In the summer of 1978 I participated in a panel discussion on Soviet Jewry at Temple B'Nai Israel in Oklahoma City. During the evening a member of the audience complained that too many Soviet Jews, when they *do* get permission to leave their homeland, come to the United States rather than go to Israel. After a moment of awkward silence, Rabbi David Packman turned to the speaker and said softly: "But aren't we here because our own fathers and grandfathers made that same choice?"

Of course. Almost all of us are here for that same reason. The melting pot has never completely melted us—nor should it. Blacks are not the only Americans consciously aware of their roots. It is amazing, then, that this nation of ethnics—Scots, Irish, Poles, Lithuanians, Germans, Swedes, Swiss and all the rest—should find itself becoming increasingly hostile toward "them", the "foreigners." It is not unusual for me to hear constituents who themselves escaped to America from Nazi or Communist persecution now complain bitterly about the influx of people "who don't even speak English."

There are a number of reasons why this transformation has taken place. And it *is* a transformation. During World War II, when this country overreacted against native Americans of Japanese descent and placed them in special camps, great numbers of Americans were outraged—and many more have become ashamed in retrospect as the great contributions and loyalties of Japanese-Americans have become evident. Yet today the same nation that is embarrassed by that inexcusable indignity, is almost ready to build a wall tall enough to hide the inviting inscription on the Statue of Liberty.

"Your poor, your tired, your hungry? Send them someplace else. We've got all we can handle."

It's true, of course, that there has always been a hostility toward new arrivals, no matter what Emma Lazarus said. Jews were barred from many places. The Italians resented the Irish; the Irish resented the blacks; the blacks resented the Puerto Ricans. Jobs were scarce at the bottom of the ladder, and competition wasn't welcome.

Today, however, the hostility is not localized among lower-income groups. Americans at all income levels find reason to "keep the foreigners out."

The reasons are varied.

At a time when the economy is tight and people are frustrated (a dangerous time in any nation), Americans have found themselves inundated with thousands of new arrivals. First it was the Cubans escaping from Castro and bringing great changes in southern Florida. Then it was the Vietnamese, fleeing from certain execution at the hands of the Communists. They were not serious competition in the job market for most Americans, but they were definitely new burdens on a people already overtaxed. Unlike earlier immigrants, they came at the taxpayer's expense.

And that has been a major part of the growing hostility. New arrivals have come as new burdens. Especially illegal immigrants, most from Mexico and South America. And students.

And the student influx brought another special problem. Many of the new foreign students were from the Middle East, especially from Iran. It was bad enough that Americans, suffering already from the humiliation (and economic squeeze) caused by dependence on Middle East oil producers, had to watch oil-wealthy playboys squander great fortunes on wildly-painted statues and mansions; what was worse, the newcomers took their political battles into the streets of American cities. In Oklahoma City, Iranians belted their fellow students—and police officers—with chairs during a melee at a small college and then violated city and state laws by demonstrating in hooded uniforms reminiscent of the Ku Klux Klan.

Of course it is possible to understand the motivations in some cases. So-called "wetbacks" come to the United States because there is more opportunity here (and because some American businessmen welcome such low-cost labor). Iranian students protested because the Shah was a dictator; they protested here, in disguise, because it would have been dangerous to do otherwise.

But the combined effect of rioting Iranians, aliens receiving welfare checks and American taxpayers footing the bill for relocating fleeing foreigners had its effect on public thinking, and it is clearly one reason for the frightening re-emergence of the KKK. In times of unrest, the frightened and "threatened" are easy prey for Hitlers and Klansmen.

The reaction has been heightened by a sudden escalation in the amount of foreign investment in this country. Americans reading national magazines learn that farmland, hotels, restaurants are being gobbled up by Arab investors, Dutch investors, Canadian investors, Japanese investors. It is something that has never happened here before, and it is a disturbing new experience.

Businessmen familiar with international trade argue that an overreaction on our part (prohibiting certain foreign investments, for example) could result in counter-measures against American investors and American products. They argue that changes in markets have made others wealthy, but with limited avenues for investing their money in their own countries. They argue that investment by foreigners in this country is not a precursor to a foreign takeover but rather a foreign vote of confidence in the American economy (and a move that gives these non-Americans incentive to make sure the United States remains economically strong).

But these are arguments that often fall on deaf ears. Americans suddenly begin to see "foreigners" everywhere—not in a steady flow of hungry immigrants into the big Eastern cities, but in a rush of foreign students, foreign investors, foreign welfare recipients. The result is fear.

The resultant hostility is still sub-surface and not widely discussed, but it is there and the patterns are beginning to develop. They may result in new economic sanctions against foreign imports; in a narrowing of immigration quotas, in prohibitions against foreign investment; in local decisions not to accept as many foreign students in American colleges and universities. And each action may produce a responsive reaction by the countries affected. We are not the only nation able to impose tariffs.

I do not yet know what form the American protest ultimately will take, but it is an emerging reality that demands the government's attention. The alternative may well be an upheaval with grave and barely foreseeable consequences.

Part Three
AN AGENDA FOR THE 80s

CHAPTER EIGHT
INADEQUACY AND EXCLUSION: THE FAILURES OF THE 70s, THE PROBLEMS OF THE 80s

1. Energy and Education, Aging and Assimilation

Critical problems exist that we must finally face up to in the 1980s—problems ranging from the inadequacy of our public education system to the inadequacy of our foreign policy, the exclusion of blacks from the American economic system and the growing disregard for basic constitutional rights in a modern society that is increasingly dominated by a relatively autonomous bureaucracy.

Unless America honestly addresses and does something about the deteriorating quality of its public schools, it will increasingly produce adult generations incapable of communicating clearly, mastering the complex technology of the late 20th century or providing intellectual leadership for the future.

Unless America addresses and solves its awesome energy problems, it will find itself unable in the 1980s to sustain that complex technology, unable to maintain its national security, unable to provide jobs for its people.

Unless America finally begins to assimilate its black population into the economic mainstream of society, it will find itself faced with renewed racial tension as millions of citizens find that their expectations and their aspirations for the future simply cannot be fulfilled by the "table scraps" theories of liberal white and black politicians.

Unless America concerns itself with the almost imperceptible growth of its non-elected government and the power that government has to simply ignore the Bill of Rights when it's convenient to do so, America may well survive but it won't be the same place.

And there are other problems as well:

Women must be assimilated into the upper levels of the free enterprise system.

Unless energy shortages force an unexpected reversal of trends, Americans can expect great technological advances throughout the remainder of the 20th century, including better and faster means of transportation and communication. Can we continue to adopt new technologies without further diminishing the quality of life? Or are we all destined to become numbers and codes funneled into countless categories and sorted by ever-more complex computers?

Will we cope with the ever-advancing age of our population by finding ways to keep older Americans involved in society or will we persist in the absurd and inexcusable trend to force early retirement and shunt our senior citizens off to the sidelines?

Can we build a defense system strong enough to defend our free society without destroying the freedoms that make that society worth defending?

The list goes on and on and a score of books could not address all the problems that have to be faced. But most of these problems—as critical as they are, for different reasons—have this in common: Not much is being done about any of them.

For example:

The education establishment continues to dig in its heels and resists scattered efforts—mostly by journalists and parents—to force change. Television newsman Edwin Newman has written books calling public attention to the inability of many Americans to use the English language; a professor at Glassboro State College in New Jersey started a small newspaper, *The Underground Grammarian,* to take people to task for butchering the tools of communication; newspaper and magazine writers have produced extensive reports about the consistent decline in student scores on achievement tests. Yet for each of these failings professional educators make excuses. The education unions have failed to do anything about, and apparently to care very much about, the fact that many of their members can't read or write very well, and aren't doing a very good job of teaching our children to read or write, either. And politicians from Bangor to Butte avoid the issue, out of a very real fear of the political power of the National Educational Association, the American Federation of Teachers, and the various state affiliates of both unions.

Much of the energy debate has centered on the battle between those who favor increased production and those who favor increased environmental protection. For a time it has centered on the debate over whether producers of oil and natural gas should be given greater incentives to explore, drill, refine, transport and market their products. There have been scattered and occasional debates about how to finance the development of alternate energy sources—solar, geothermal, clean coal, grain conversion.

But the real energy issue in America centers on whether or not this country is going to increase its reliance on nuclear power as the primary energy source for the near future. And virtually no one is debating the issue in a responsible way.

All reason seems to have been suspended in consideration of the nuclear issue. America has divided into two camps: "No Nukes" and "Go Nukes." Those who are *anti*-nuclear seem to have the same fear of nuclear power-generating facilities that children have of the dark. Their minds are effectively closed on the matter.

Those who are *pro*-nuclear find nuclear power plants, with their leaks, their cracks, their control-panel breakdowns, still as safe and harmless and lovable as cotton candy or a cocker spaniel puppy. Even to suggest that there ought to be an evacuation plan for nuclear disasters, like the ones we have for floods, is as un-American as Patton slapping out a battle-weary soldier.

There are people in America who are decidedly pro-nuclear but who think we ought to try to make nuclear plants as safe as possible *before* we build them, not after. But they are few in number and nobody pays much attention to them.

The "black problem" in America is a problem precisely because it continues to be viewed primarily in a racial context. The problem, however, has moved beyond that stage, and while there are unquestionably vestiges of discrimination, whether overt or subtle, the real problem today is the fact that a sizeable part of the potential free enterprise workforce remains outside the private, productive, sector of the economy. Which is a problem for all of us.

Almost all of the attempts to help blacks overcome the effects of racial discrimination have been of the breadline variety. Parren Mitchell, a black Congressman from Maryland, explained to me one afternoon on the House floor that this concentration on "make-work" solutions is because any attempt to seriously deal with the problems of minority America must include not only a long-term approach but also a short-term approach, which requires doing something about the immediate crisis: how to pay this month's heating bill, for example.

While the government continues to seek ways to meet those short-term emergencies, however, black liberals, who sometimes seem to be more concerned with liberal dogma than with black needs, continue to ignore and even oppose efforts to devise a long-range strategy that will at some foreseeable time virtually erase all racial distinctions in America and have blacks so thoroughly integrated into the society that such things as a "black political agenda" will be as unnecessary and redundant as the existence of a "white political agenda" or a "Lutheran political agenda" or an "Elks Lodge political agenda."

America must reorient its thinking toward the blacks and other minorities in its midst and begin to make it possible—as it has never done—for meaningful numbers of minorities to achieve secure positions within the free enterprise system at the employee level, at the managerial level and at the ownership level.

Then, and only then, will the young black child be able to look forward to the same kind of future many white youngsters take for granted. And then, and only then, will the divisions between "black America" and "white America" be healed.

The increased powers of the bureaucracy? Well, that issue is of a different kind altogether, partly because the problem has come upon us so quietly that few seem aware of its scope.

When most people who complain about the bureaucracy do so it is usually as an objection to a specific federal rule or regulation that affects them directly in their business or personal life. When politicians complain about the bureaucracy generally, it is usually about the enormous cost of sustaining that bureaucracy and the many bureaucratic absurdities that fit so well into a civic club speech.

But the greatest problem is not with specific regulations or wasted money or institutionalized inanity. The greatest problem is with the powers that have begun to accrue to those agencies.

While each of these problem areas embodies a complex pattern of causes, effects and potential improvements, dealing with all of them here would turn a relatively thin book into a paperweight worthy of Clavell or Michener. Instead, I will concentrate on looking more closely at just a few of the problems that dominate the political agenda of the 80s.

2. Beyond the Fifth Amendment: The Growing Power of the Federal Bureaucracy

In recent years regulations and decisions by federal agencies have repeatedly provoked massive public reaction: to the Food and Drug Administration's attempt to outlaw saccharin; the Treasury Department's attempt to impose handgun registration in defiance of the Congress; proposed IRS regulations to remove the tax-exempt status of private schools and to alter the "independent contractor" tax status of real estate agents. Each of these attempts has given rise to an outpouring of mail demanding that the Congress block the new rulings.

There is little doubt that the growth of the federal bureaucracy has become one of the greatest dangers facing the continued existence of the free enterprise economic system. Today, every businessman, whether he operates a day-care center, a funeral home, a bookstore, a small oil company, a bank, a laundry, a small manufacturing plant, or any other enterprise, finds himself not only buried under federal paperwork but subject also to an increasing number of rules, regulations and guidelines for the manufacture, packaging, labeling, distribution and inventory of almost every product on the market.

But as a teacher of administrative law in the law school at Oklahoma City University I found my attention directed not only to the more obvious excesses of the bureaucracy, but also to the enormous powers now residing in federal agencies, powers which literally allow bureaucrats to avoid the constraints of the federal constitution: the power to conduct search and seizure without a warrant; to require persons to give testimony against themselves; to subject citizens to hearings without giving them the right to confront their accusers—all violations of basic rights which are essential to our constitutional form of government.

A brief test:

The United States Constitution protects us from having our homes, offices, cars or persons searched unless the authorities have a search warrant. True or False?

In the United States we can't be punished for violating a law unless we've had a chance to be heard, to cross-examine people who are accusing us, to confront our accusers. True or false?

If you answered "true" to both questions you would probably get an A in any highschool civics course. But you'd be in deep trouble in the real world.

The truth is, the government *does* search without search warrants. The government *does* seize our private papers without a warrant. The government *does* punish Americans every day without giving them a hearing or the right to confront or cross-examine the people who accuse them.

And about that Fifth Amendment that most mobsters know so well—the right not to incriminate oneself? Thousands of Americans every year are forced, legally, by their government to incriminate themselves.

Is this in some deep rural backwoods courtroom, where a tyrannical judge ignores the citizen's constitutional rights? No, it's in federal buildings throughout America, and too often the courts have held that we don't have any of those rights at all, at least not when we're dealing with a federal agency.

And about that Fifth Amendment that most mobsters know so well—the right not to incriminate oneself? Thousands of Americans every year are forced legally by their government to incriminate themselves.

Is this in some deep rural backwoods courtroom, where a tyrannical judge ignores the citizen's constitutional rights? No, it's in federal buildings throughout America, and too often the courts have held that we don't have any of those rights at all, at least not when we're dealing with a federal agency.

And more and more Americans are dealing with federal agencies every day. Most of us are aware of the rapid growth in the numbers of federal agencies, the increasing amount of tax dollars they spend, and the growing army of federal bureaucrats it takes to keep the agencies running. Fewer people are aware, however, of the large and growing number of citizens who find themselves regulated, harassed and fined by federal agencies. And fewer still are aware that when most citizens enter the murky world of conflict with the federal bureaucracy they leave many of their constitutional protections behind.

For the average American the administrative process can be frightening: final decisions that can destroy a business can be made by men who have not heard, or read, any of the testimony; persons accused of violating federal regulations can be denied the right to question their accusers or even to know who they are, and they can even be denied the right to be heard in their own behalf, eliminating a basic protection that was preserved even in the notorious Star Chamber trials of Europe's Dark Ages.

As I have studied administrative law, I have become increasingly aware that this is an area in which the rule of law simply does not apply—an area in which hundreds of thousands of decisions which affect millions of people are made under inconsistent and often unfair procedures. Agency decisions, for example, need not follow precedent; they can be completely inconsistent with earlier decisions on the same subject by the same agency. "Due process" is written off, thanks to a Supreme Court decision, as meaning whatever process is due "in light of the circumstances."

The Supreme Court, in fact, has been overly generous in permitting federal agencies to avoid the constraints of the federal constitution. Over the years the Court has sanctioned a growing list of awesome bureaucratic powers:

Does the Fourth Amendment guarantee that no American shall be subject to unreasonable searches and seizures? The Court has ruled that the Fourth Amendment sometimes does not apply when that search or seizure is by a federal agency.

The Fifth Amendment doesn't apply to your business records if an administrative agency requires you to keep them.

A federal agency can search your company records without giving any reason at all; simple curiosity is enough. (One agency, in fact, demanded that a bank over which it had no jurisdiction turn over its records concerning the account of a customer over whom the agency had no jurisdiction. The bank had to comply.)

In his book, *The First Circle*, Aleksandr Solzhenitsyn described the ordeal of a prisoner in the notorious Lubyanka prison: "Each time, and always for a different reason, they asked him to do something that seemed inconsequential compared with the major battle that lay ahead—and each time it seemed not worth being stubborn about something so trivial. But the total effect of this procedure was to break the prisoner's will completely."

It's the same principle, obviously, as what occurs when single drops of water over a protracted period of time succeed in wearing a hole through solid rock. And it's the same way in which the powers of the bureaucracy have grown, with the gradual erosion—one drop at a time, by one agency or another, by one court decision or another—of the basic constitutional safeguards with which Americans become familiar in elementary school classrooms.

As a result, the powers of federal agencies have grown so enormously that one legal scholar—an expert in the ever-more-liberal interpretation of administrative law—wryly observed that "the remnants of constitutional principles are left standing, but only to an extent consistent with permitting administrative agencies to secure the materials they need." Or want.

This tremendous bureaucratic power is made worse by the rapid growth in the size, scope and number of federal agencies.

In 1947, *Clark's Summary of American Law* devoted only 11 pages to Administrative Law—one-sixth as much as it gave to Torts, half of what it gave to Trusts, to Corporations, to Conflicts of Jurisdiction.

By 1952, five years later, as the United States was emerging into the post-war world of burgeoning government, federal agencies had expanded so rapidly that Supreme Court Justice Robert Jackson wrote: "The rise of administrative bodies probably has been the most significant legal trend of the last century and perhaps more values today are affected by their decisions than by those of all the courts...."

Five more years passed, and by 1957 Justice Felix Frankfurter observed: "Review of administrative action, mainly reflecting enforcement of federal regulatory statutes, constitutes the largest category of the courts' work, comprising one-third of the total cases decided on the merits."

By 1960, Justice Tom Clark observed that: "Administrative law is now the most important body of law...."

Professor Kenneth Davis, one of the nation's leading administrative law scholars, wrote: "The average person is much more directly and much more frequently affected by the administrative process than by the judicial process. The ordinary person probably regards the judicial process as somewhat remote from his own problems; a large portion of all people go through life without ever being party to a lawsuit. But the administrative process affects nearly everyone in many ways nearly every day."

This growth in the importance—and enormous reach—of administrative law is visible in concrete terms. By the end of the fiscal year ending June 30, 1963, by which time the trend toward bureaucratic decision-making had firmly established itself (and even before much of the recent proliferation of federal agencies), the number of civil trials in all the federal district courts in all the states combined was 7,095. By contrast, the number of *formal cases* disposed of by federal agencies was 81,469—more than 11 times the number of federal court trials. (And that was only those cases which included a formal hearing and a prepared verbatim transcript—only a small fraction of the decisions made by the bureaucracy. For example, during one recent year the Federal Aviation Administration investigated more than 3,000 reports of air safety violations and suspended 1,500 certificates, but held only 107 formal hearings.)

Reading the *Federal Register* to keep up with new federal regulations has become a vital daily activity for national organizations representing almost every category of business. And as the number of regulations increases, so does the number of agency "trials."

As long ago as 1916, leaders of the legal profession began to warn of the dangers inherent in the rapid growth of bureaucratic power. In that year Elihu Root, then the president of the American Bar Association and later Secretary of State, warned: "If we are to continue a government of limited powers, these agencies of regulation must themselves be regulated. . . the rights of the citizens against them must be made plain."

By 1932, James Beck, a former solicitor general in the Justice Department, warned that "Uncle Sam has not yet awakened from his dream of government by bureaucracy, but ever wanders further afield in crazy experiments. . . ."

By 1938, halfway through Franklin D. Roosevelt's New Deal, with its increased emphasis on the use of federal agencies to promote the administration's policies, the "dream of government by bureaucracy" was rapidly becoming a nightmare. Dean Roscoe Pound, one of the most respected legal scholars in American history, was appointed by the American Bar Association to head a special committee on administrative law. In his report, Pound warned that administrative agencies were showing a tendency to decide without a hearing, to hear only one side, and to make decisions on the basis of pre-formed opinions and prejudices.

These warnings and many others led in 1946 to the passage of the federal Administrative Procedures Act. The act itself stirred a furious debate in the Congress—not due to any disagreement over whether administrative agencies need to be regulated but because many in the Congress feared that while imposing some modest restraints on federal agencies, the Act, by its existence, would legitimize the concept of having such agencies at all, a matter that was then still very much in dispute because of the arbitrary way in which agencies exercised their powers.

In 1955, when a task force on regulatory commissions called on the Congress to tighten the Administrative Procedures Act, Attorney General Herbert Brownell protested that the change would have "disastrous results to *efficient and effective government.*"

That of course, raises the central question: what is more important in a free society: justice or "efficiency"?

The more efficient a government, the greater a threat it poses to the freedom of its citizens and the more difficult for them to act with confidence that they are safe from the law. A proper balance is therefore required: a government that is reasonably efficient but bound by necessity to follow carefully prescribed procedures and to observe mandatory safeguards.

Unfortunately, administrative law has gone beyond that point and has developed into an often arbitrary method of imposing the government will on the individual in ways that he is often helpless to defend against.

It is common practice for members of Congress to defend themselves against the complaints of constituents by arguing that the action of government which has upset them is the fault of some federal agency or another, and not the fault of the Congress. To some extent that is an evasion of responsibility, because the Congress, when it creates any federal agency, has the power—and a responsibility—to impose sufficient guidelines and restraints to prevent the bureaucracy from abusing the powers delegated to it. But delegation of powers without any constraints at all has become standard practice, and today the federal courts freely permit the Congress and the executive branch to delegate awesome powers without even the most elementary standards or guidelines. Power is delegated down, down, down, to cabinet secretaries, agency heads, regional directors, and at each step the holder of the delegated power assumes frightening decision-making authority which it is expensive, and often fruitless, to challenge.

The discretionary power of federal agencies is often used as a club. For example, when President Nixon established wage and price controls, the first phase included absolutely no prohibitions at all concerning the issuance of stock dividends. Nonetheless, when six major companies issued stock dividends higher than in the previous year, the administration fired off telegrams protesting the increases and called representatives of the companies to a meeting at the White House. The Cost of Living Council then issued a press release attacking the companies and announcing that they had been summoned to Washington to explain their actions against the national interest. The companies backed down. Perhaps the result was a good one, but it clearly illustrates the possibilities for the harsh use of such discretionary power.

Professor Davis, arguing for elimination of excessive discretion, warned about not only "the cancerous growth of unnecessary discretionary power," but especially about the "power of selective enforcement"—the power to choose *which* person or companies to go after, another mighty club with which agencies force private citizens to bend to the will of the government.

This concern, which I share with Professor Davis, led me to remind my students frequently during my teaching days that an attorney's proper function with regard to the government is not to promote government efficiency but to protect his client from that efficiency.

The list of bureaucratic abuses is lengthy and impressive.

Each agency may establish its own procedures for obtaining evidence, and the procedures thus vary greatly, forcing citizens to shop for highly specialized—and very expensive—attorneys, familiar not only with administrative procedure but with the unique procedure of a single agency.

Although it is commonly assumed that agencies must publish their rules in the *Federal Register* before they can be adopted, agencies have the right to adopt rules without publishing them if the agency decides that publication is either not necessary or not convenient.

A federal agency may deny a citizen the opportunity even to submit facts and arguments in an adjudicatory proceeding (a trial) in which he may be cited, fined, punished, perhaps even forced out of business.

An agency decision may be totally inconsistent with previous decisions.

An agency official may make a decision completely on his own—for any reasons he wishes—without talking to the agency officials who heard the testimony in the case.

And the citizen can't even appeal to the courts until he has "exhausted his administrative remedies," a step-by-step procedure through the bureaucracy that can entangle a company or individual in costly legal procedures for years—a prime reason why so many just give up and agree to whatever fine or punishment the agency chooses; in the long run, it's cheaper.

We should make basic changes in the law to give citizens the same basic protections when they go before a federal agency that they would have in a courtroom.

I have attempted to meet at least part of the problem by introducing legislation to bring about a major overhaul of the federal Administrative Procedures Act. My proposed legislation would:

1. Require an agency to publish detailed descriptions of the standards and principles which govern its discretionary decisions.

2. Require federal agencies to publish in the Federal Register all interpretive rules and statements of policy adopted by the agency.

3. Eliminate the agency's discretion to adopt rules without publication.

4. Require an agency to provide an opportunity for oral arguments, pro and con, on proposed rule making.

5. Provide that substantive rules be published in the Federal Register at least 120 days before their effective date.

6. Provide that no rule required to be published in the Federal Register shall take effect until approved by each committee of the Congress having jurisdiction with respect to the agency involved.

7. Remove an agency's option to deny a party the opportunity to submit facts and arguments in adjudicatory (trial) proceedings.

8. Provide that a witness, party, or other person required to submit data or evidence shall be entitled to retain a copy or transcript and shall be entitled to purchase a copy of any data or evidence submitted by any other witness, party, or person. (Amazingly, they don't now have that right).

9. State that no officer or employee of any agency may enter any property for the purposes of inspection, search, or seizure, except upon authority of a search warrant issued by a court of competent jurisdiction.

10. Require all Federal agencies to adopt the Federal Rules of Evidence to assure uniformity in procedure.

When I was a student in law school, one of my professors, Wayne Quinlan, frequently reminded his classes that any similarity between justice and the law was purely accidental. This legislation, aimed at reducing the powers of the federal bureaucracy and restoring basic constitutional protections to the individual citizen, can go a long way toward bringing the law and justice together. It will not address the larger problem—the problem of reducing the scope of government regulation—but at least it would move toward a system in which American citizens would have basic legal protections when they are challenged by a federal agency.

3. The Decline of Public Education

The last several years have seen a rapid and uninterrupted decline in the quality of public education.

There are many reasons offered to explain *why* this is so, but for whatever reason, it *is* so. The America of the 1980s will be able to maintain neither its own standards of excellence nor its position of international leadership unless the trend is reversed.

Examples of the decline are depressingly plentiful.

Paul Copperman, in his 1978 book, *The Literacy Hoax*, compared student performance on Scholastic Aptitude Tests (SATs), on a yearly basis, during the period from 1952 through 1977. During that period, the average math score increased from 494 in 1952 to a peak of 502 in 1963, and then dropped sharply and steadily each year thereafter; by the last year of the study (1977) the average score had dropped to 470. Verbal aptitude scores increased very slightly from 476 in 1952 to 478, the peak (again, in 1963), and then dropped precipitously, alarmingly, year after year, to 429 in 1977.

Copperman concluded "With skills down, assignments down, standards down, and grades up, the American educational system perpetrates a hoax on its students and on their parents."

Copperman's findings have been repeatedly confirmed. The National Assessment of Educational Progress, for example, found that one-fourth of America's 17-year-old students cannot multiply 671 by 402 and get the right answer. (One recent high school graduate working in a restaurant in Oklahoma City, had difficulty figuring out how much my son and I owed for our meals—a task which required adding five charges, the largest of which was $4.95. Finally she had to use a calculator.)

Average scores on scholastic aptitude tests taken by high school seniors declined still further in the years after Copperman concluded his study. By 1979, the average score in the testing of verbal skills was only 427 points out of a possible 800 (two points lower than in the last year Copperman measured).

The lowest possible score on the test was 200; therefore the average score (only 227 points above the minimum) was less than 38 percent of the potential score (600 points above minimum)—a clear and undeniable "F", although grading "on the curve" (comparing, rather than measuring achievement) would cause a score of 427 to earn a "C".

It is precisely this way, incidentally, in the classroom, where grades are often determined on the curve, that as average scores go down, lower and lower scores are required to "pass." One year a 75 may earn a "C"; a few years later, with everybody's score lower, a student may need only a score of 70 to earn a "C", since to earn a "C" his work need only be average in comparison with everyone else's. As a result, some students are graduated each year knowing less than even the least-informed graduate of the year before.

Not only are overall test scores declining, but such teaching failures are having a serious detrimental impact on individual lives. For example, at the Oklahoma City CETA training center at which young people without skills were trained in an effort to help them get jobs, officials reported that applicants who had high school diplomas often could read only at a third-or fourth-grade level, and thus had difficulty learning job skills.

In his book, Copperman describes the ordeal of a student who was graduated from high school despite the expressed concern of his parents, who felt he had not learned to read very well. When the young man received his first job, which required only a minimum amount of paperwork, he lasted only a few weeks. He sued the state for the inadequacy of his education. He did not prevail—to the relief of the education establishment—but the point was made: he remains severely handicapped in a highly competitive world because people who were paid to teach him failed in their jobs.

It was interesting to listen to the comments of students interviewed on Oklahoma City radio stations during a strike by teachers in 1979. As the community debated whether or not the teachers should be paid more, high school students complained: "Them substitutes aren't doing a good job."

Cartoonist Jules Feiffer made the point well in a cartoon published October 21, 1979, in the *Washington Star*. In the cartoon, a young adult asks a small child: "Where you running to?" The child answers: "I'm late to school."

Adult: "What's your first class?"

Child: "Sex education."

Adult: "Learned your math yet?"

Child: "No."

Adult: "Learned your history yet?"

Child: "No."

Adult: "Learned your science yet?"

Child: "No."

Adult: "Can you read yet?"

Child: "No."

Adult: "Maybe you better learn sex in the streets."

Cartoonist Jim Lange of the *Daily Oklahoman* made the same point in a drawing showing an angry teacher on a picket line. Her sign proclaimed: "Teechurs against..."

Is such sharp criticism unfair? A photograph on the front page of the *Oklahoman* showed a *real* graduate teaching assistant marching in a picket line. On her sign she had written: "The kid at MacDonald's earns more than your English teacher."

Maybe. And if he does, it's a disgrace. But at least he knows how to spell "McDonald's," which is more, apparently, than this prospective teacher knew.

One reason for this diminished quality of education is clear. In recent years there has been a tendency to fill the hours a student spends at school with "relevant" courses that teach the child to sew, bake and dribble a basketball.

I do not contend that these non-academic courses have no place in our schools, but there must be some attempt made to keep things in perspective. One of my stepsons attended a high school in northern Virginia. He was required to take a course in physical education. The section he preferred, which would have involved physical activity, was full, so he was assigned to a section on "Fundamentals of Football." He and the other students used this time to watch football films and listen—or sleep—as a coach (teacher) explained the finer points of the game. (Which, of course, removes the essential reason for requiring PE courses in the first place—to enhance physical fitness.) That semester he received one high school credit for watching football films, one credit for English, and one credit for history. Apparently the school system considered the courses of equal importance.

To a very large extent, the declining quality of public education stems from the inadequate education of teachers themselves. For example, a recently published study by a researcher at Boston University indicates that departments of education in American colleges have lowered their standards for admission and for graduation.

A study of tests taken by college seniors majoring in education found that on the verbal parts of the tests these future teachers scored a full 25 points below the average for majors in other fields. They scored 51 points below average on the mathematics portion of the test.

The Washington Post reported that a teacher in Virginia wrote to a university to ask "weather" a course would be beneficial to him. In Washington, a high school teacher began a lecture about civil rights by writing the topic on the blackboard. She spelled it: "Civille Right."

(To be fair I should recognize that this lowering of standards may be due in part to a shortage of teaching jobs and unforgivably low starting salaries for teachers, both of which make it harder for schools to find enough people willing to major in education. But to be *completely* fair, I should also point out that as long ago as 1958, when I was a senior at the University of Oklahoma, I was one of several students who, having completed all the course requirements for graduation, and needing only more credit hours, decided to enroll in some "snap" courses for easy "A's". We chose a senior-level education course, though none of us had ever taken any other education courses, and spent the semester earnestly debating whether schools should "teach" or help students adjust to society. At the end of the semester, we received our "A's," although most of us had not shown great promise academically during the previous years when we enrolled in non-education courses. Either we had all come to a late flowering or it is not fully accurate to suggest that the education of educators is just now showing deficiencies.)

Because graduates in education now apparently know less than their predecessors (or their contemporaries who are enrolled in other disciplines), one could assume they are getting out of school with lower grades—just barely getting by. That, of course, is to imagine that there is some correlation between learning and grades. However, in the spring semester of 1977, at the University of Houston, 93 percent of the grades given to all elementary education seniors were either "A's" or B's." The great majority (70 percent) were "A's." It seems one must really be a dud *not* to make an "A" or "B" in education courses these days. (I know that's harsh language, and I do not think society can fairly lay all the blame for the low quality of public education at the feet of the teachers. But we are talking about my son's future, my daughter's future—*your* son's or daughter's future.) According to *Newsweek*, "more than 23 million Americans—one out of every five adults—cannot read, write or compute well enough to function effectively in today's world" and another 40 million "possess just the minimal skills necessary for survival." This is important business.

The results of this education deficiency are shocking. One-half of 535 first-year teachers in the Dallas public school system failed a test to determine if they were qualified to teach. (Unfortunately, when they took the test, they were *already* teaching.) The teachers failed to achieve a standard described generously by *Texas Monthly Magazine* as "far from rigorous." In fact, it was what we used to call a "pud" test—a real snap. It required knowing things like: *"fish is to water as bird is to air."* Juniors and seniors in a private high school made far better scores on the same test.

In Houston, half the education graduates who applied for teaching jobs scored lower in mathematical achievement than any high school junior who took the test.

In two counties in Maryland, half the teachers who applied for jobs failed proficiency examinations.

At Southwest Texas State Teachers College, which turns out more teachers than any other college or university in the state, not one student—*not one*—in a class of senior education majors knew who had written *War and Peace.*

Texas Monthly asked: "What happened to the era, not so long ago, really, when teachers were rightfully respected as the best-educated people in the community? And now they can't outperform high school juniors. How has it come to this?"

Early in 1980 the *New York Times* published an article entitled "1978 Freshmen Score Poorly on 1928 Exam." The article reported on a study by Dr. Alvin C. Eurich, former acting president of Stanford University and Chancellor of the State University of New York. To Dr. Eurich, the *Times* reported, the results demonstrated "that freshmen today cannot cover as much ground in a given time as students half a century ago, or comprehend what they read as well."

Christopher Jencks, a professor of sociology at Harvard, examined the trend in a thoughtful article in *Working Papers.* He began by reviewing the discoveries of a host of indicators:

"Five years ago," he wrote, "the College Entrance Examination Board announced that college applicants' scores on the Scholastic Aptitude Test (SAT) were declining. Shortly thereafter American College Testing, which tests almost all college applicants who do not take the SAT, reported a similar decline. Since then, the National Assessment of Educational Progress (NAEP) has announced that 17-year-olds as a group knew less about the natural sciences, wrote worse essays, made less accurate inferences from what they read, and were less adept at using reference works in 1973-74 than in 1969-70. Last winter, NAEP reported that students' knowledge about politics had also declined. Iowa's statewide testing program, which provides detailed annual data on a stable population, shows steady declines since 1966 in vocabulary, quantitative thinking, ability to look things up, ability to express oneself, and knowledge of literature, social studies, and the natural sciences. These declines are found at all high school grades and in the upper elementary school grades. Minnesota eleventh graders' scores on the state's scholastic aptitude test have also fallen. McGraw-Hill's Comprehensive Tests of Basic Skills (CTBS) show a nationwide decline in reading, language, and math between 1968 and 1973 for students in grades six through ten.''

Professor Jencks' article is no polemic; he goes to great lengths to point out a number of his more encouraging findings: For example, he says, "The national decline among high school seniors did not begin until the 1960s, and it is as yet far less than the earlier gain. It is still safe to assume that the average student today knows more than his or her parents knew at the same age." He emphasizes that there are a number of factors which have contributed to the decline, and that there may be questions as to the validity of the tests themselves. But his own conclusions point to an even broader concern:

"Where older students run into trouble is in making inferences from what they read. They know what a passage says, but they do not understand what the author's point really is. When they write they make no more spelling or punctuation mistakes than 17-year-olds made a few years ago, but they turn out less coherent paragraphs. The trouble, then, is not with ''the basics'' but with what for lack of a better term we might call 'complex' skills. But skills are not the only problem. Today's high school graduates have not read as widely as their predecessors, are at least they do not seem to know as much about the kinds of things young people traditionally learned from reading. They do worse on tests that ask about literature, history, politics, and scientific subjects. And they do not seem to think as carefully about the problems testers set for them, even when the solution does not require external information."

Dr. Jencks is a respected member of the academic community, and his work is scholarly. There are, however, other, less lofty, indicators of the problem. The Big Sky Conference announced in 1979, for example, that it would not have an all-academic football team that year, because not enough athletes qualified.

As the education establishment continues to ignore the deteriorating quality of its product, private citizens have begun to speak up in loud complaint.

Leslie Braunstein, a communications manager for a consulting firm in Maryland, wrote to the *Washington Post* after seeing the now-familiar bumper sticker, "If you can read this, thank your teacher."

"I'm convinced," she wrote, that "my former teachers owe me more than I owe them. For my basic ability to read and write, I thank a devoted 'unofficial' teacher: my mother. Before I was old enough for nursery school, she had me reading 'Alice and Jerry' books and writing poetry. These activities keep us both amused until I entered grade school, where I learned to endure lessons in the things I already knew. I was never allowed to move ahead of the group to do challenging work; it was more important to be 'emotionally adjusted' as part of the mainstream."

She described one teacher who stood out as helpful to her, and concluded: "He's one of the few teachers I can thank when I'm faced with a problem more challenging than reading a bumper sticker."

Blacks who still have greater obstacles to overcome than most other Americans in trying to achieve some sort of success and security, are painfully aware of their need for a quality education to enable them to break into the predominantly white economic system.

In an editorial in the *Washington Post* in November, 1979, columnist William Raspberry, a black, wrote:

"We are not teaching our children to use the language. If local school administrators understood that, they might join me in a campaign to smash every ditto machine in the school system. Even the best schools in town keep sending their children home with those purple ditto sheets on which they are to fill in blanks as evidence that they have read and digested their assignments.

"...They are, in fact, evidence of nothing, except the ability of youngsters to scan a chapter in search of the appropriate sentences and to copy down the missing words and phrases.

"...The problem for the D.C. public schools," he wrote, "is...to teach, to stop handing out grades as compensation for poverty."

In Chicago, Marva Collins, a black teacher, has established a private school for inner-city children. She refuses all federal funds and insists on a curriculum built around the basics:

"If you can't read," she says, "you can't do anything else. I can't see why society finds this so difficult to understand."

William Raspberry and Marva Collins are not alone in understanding the special importance a good education can have for black youngsters.

Black civil rights leader Bayard Rustin, interviewed for Peter Joseph's book, *Good Times*, complained about what he called "remnants of stupidity":

"Like the Ford Foundation giving one hundred thousand dollars to study black English, as if there is any such thing. There is just bad Southern English, which blacks and whites speak. You can't make anything of it except that it's just bad...one of our problems for Negroes is that we do not have the language, reading and mathematics tools for existing in this society..."

Syndicated columnist Carl Rowan, another prominent black, put it this way:

"What black children need is not the right to go their own linguistic way in the name of 'black pride'. What they need is an end to this malarkey that tells them they can fail to learn grammar, fail to develop vocabularies, ignore syntax and embrace the mumbo-jumbo of ignorance."

And Milton Jordan, another black, writing in *Newsweek*, summed it up:

"Instead of opposing the competency tests, let's conquer them. Let's make sure our kids pass them."

Ironically, extensive public surveys demonstrate that the students themselves know something is missing. One prestigious report measured the attitudes of teenage students and discovered that *even they* felt they needed both more discipline and more homework.

But while many teachers clearly aren't up to the job (we all are familiar with the notices we get from teachers and principals alike containing misspelled works and incorrect grammar), it would be unfair to blame teachers and school administrators alone.

Quite obviously teachers and administrators must take *part* of the blame for the decline in the quality of education, but are they to blame when increased federalization results in teachers having to spend their time filling out federal forms instead of teaching or improving their skills? Are they to blame when school systems require teachers to spend their time organizing candy sales?

How many of us really insist that all homework be done before the children go out to play or plop down in front of the television set? How many of us have let our children put "Happy Days" and reruns of "I Love Lucy" ahead of their school work? How many of us insist that our children do *more* than was assigned in class? How many of us teach our children to behave properly? (How can teachers teach if they have to spend their time trying to maintain order in their classrooms?) How many of us insist that our children spend more time reading than watching? (I know mothers who complain because their teenage children "always have their noses buried in books." They want to know why their children aren't "normal".)

Wise parents—especially the parents of disadvantaged children—know that education may be the single most important key to a child's future. Some teachers are able to instill in their students a great love for learning, but for the most part these attitudes have to be instilled in the home. At a time when classrooms are too large and teaching is necessarily impersonal, teachers cannot be blamed if their students—and their students' parents—care too little about education.

But if the quality of public education is deplorable, and if teachers are not entirely, or primarily, to blame, what's the answer?

First, state legislators should insist that education be every state's *top* priority. A legislator who puts any state business ahead of proper support for public schools should have to make sure he has a good explanation handy.

Second, using the greater resources that would result from that decision, school board officials should see to it that teachers are paid what they are worth. (I would think that should include some sort of grading system, since not all teachers are worth the same pay.)

School officials and legislatures should give greater consideration to competency testing for students and prospective teachers. Several states now have instituted competency testing, and the American Federation of Teachers (AFL-CIO), to its great credit, has spoken in support of the concept. The largest educators union, the National Education Association, has not.

But even minimum competency testing is not enough. As John Sawhill, president of New York University, put it in an article in *Readers Digest:* "If the function of education is to enable us to become the most that we can be, there is no such thing as a minimum acceptable standard."

Schools should consider eliminating "automatic promotion" from grade to grade. The New York City school system announced that it will no longer promote or pass students automatically. They're going to start flunking some kids again.

Teachers should appoint committees of educators to sit down with PTA representatives, parents, and administrators with the sole purpose of figuring out what needs to be done to improve the quality of the education our children are receiving. Nothing else—no discussion of salaries, no discussion of tensions, no discussion of retirement benefits. Just one topic: How to see to it that those students who are graduated from our public high schools can speak intelligently, write properly, spell, read with ease, solve mathematical problems, know what countries are where, know how our government works. If they can achieve that, all of us—black, white, Hispanic, Indian, Oriental—will be better off for it. And so will our country.

4. Rethinking American Foreign Policy

Americans are directly affected every day by the quality of education in the public schools or the confrontations between labor and management that close factories, schools and football stadiums. Public attention is far less frequently focused on American initiatives in foreign policy. Unless Marines are sent to Beirut, or Americans are held captive in Teheran, or our NATO allies defy U.S.-ordered sanctions against the Soviets, international diplomacy is a matter of concern primarily to employees at the State Department and students at Georgetown University.

But in a world increasingly interdependent and increasingly threatened by pressure from the Soviet bloc, a world tormented by instability in the Middle East and Latin America, the mistakes Americans make in foreign capitals may have long lasting effects.

Under President Reagan the United States has exercised a surer hand in the international arena than it had under the hesitant and uncertain leadership of President Carter. The result has been a world which respects the United States more, and perhaps likes it less.

The direction from the Reagan White House and the rhetoric delivered at the United Nations by Ambassador Jeane Kirkpatrick have consistently focused on the use of diplomacy and power to check the aggressive nature of the Soviet Union. And that, after all, is the purpose of diplomacy: to further the security and interests of one's own nation.

It was a fact the Carter administration often forgot. Obsessed with international moralizing in relationships with the anti-Communist world, tolerant in relationships with the Communist world, the Carter foreign policy became a joke around the world and an embarrassment in the United States where even Democratic leaders in the Congress blushed at the President's ineptitude.

Clearly international decision-making is more complex than President Carter would have had us believe. When attempting to bring democratic governments to nations without democratic traditions, we must neither accept right-wing rhetoric that the nation is not suited for freedom nor expect, as the American left does, that centuries of feudalism and violence will be erased in a fortnight.

America's policy makers, if they are to be effective, must keep these complications constantly in mind. Unfortunately, however, American foreign policy—a field requiring innovative and creative thinking—has tended to become intellectually polarized.

Some argue—correctly—that it is abhorrent for the United States to support a repressive government which denies freedom to its citizens and brutally enforces its restraints. Many of the advocates of this position, however, undercut their own rhetoric about the presumption of wrongness by themselves applying their outrage selectively. Thus, it is clearly indefensible for a Somoza to act cruelly to Nicaraguans, for a South Africa to require internal passports of its black citizens, for a Taiwan to maintain members of its holdover legislature in office without challenge for more than thirty years—conclusions I agree with— but apparently, it is not equally unpleasant, for reasons I don't quite understand, for Solzhenitsyns to suffer in the Gulag or peasants to be murdered in the provinces of China. My own distaste for blind support of totalitarian or authoritarian governments is meant to be inclusive, not selective.

But the critical question is: Do facts, circumstances, sometimes justify aid to such governments, not because it is in *their* best interest, but because it is in ours?

Advocates of the "outrage theory" might doubt that circumstances would ever warrant such a decision. Unfortunately, the other polar faction in the foreign policy debate might all too often see justification in lending U.S. sanction to brutal, repressive regimes with neither moral sanction, nor the sanction of legitimacy (free elections), nor popular support. Members of the first polar group, the diplomatic moralists, were largely removed from the centers of government to the op-ed pages when President Carter was defeated. Now, the other polarity, the "Realpolitik" school (which not only sees reality but sometimes seems all too willing to accept it), has its chance to try to forge a foreign policy that, in both the short term and the long term, will be in the best interests of the United States. Unfortunately, some advocates of this diplomatic viewpoint actually seem to believe it when they hear, for example, an Eva Peron in, "Evita," promise Argentina by her statements, as she promises Juan Peron in song, "I could be surprisingly good for you."

Just as the political left selectively applies its outrage in foreign policy, the political right seems at times selectively to apply its tolerance. As we move from a sermonizing diplomacy to a foreign policy based on American self-interest, there are some essential considerations that must be kept in mind.

For the same reasons that the United States would not consider starting a war—because we operate under moral imperatives that do not constrain some other nations—we cannot, we must not, acquiesce in repression that is morally reprehensible. What is unique and wonderful about America, what makes it worth dying for, is not the fact that it exists, but the fact that it exists as a nation committed to the very principle of freedom, the belief that man's freedoms are unalienably his at birth, and that denial of those freedoms is a crime against everything we believe in. Therefore, those "imperatives" that lead us occasionally to look aside as freedoms are denied had better be imperative indeed. Herman Hesse, in his book, *Demian*, wrote that Europe had conquered the world only to lose its soul. The point is a good one: Nations, like people, can lose their souls. Posturing, preaching, and sermonizing aside, America does have a moral imperative.

Serving the long-term interests of the United States may require more sophisticated decision-making than would be necessary if we were only concerned about the state of the world, and our national security, tomorrow morning at half past nine.

Those publicly applied pressures that forced the late Shah, rapidly and under great criticism, to attempt to democratize Iran and force it, socially and politically, into the twentieth century (if American skirts and hairdos are, indeed, a mark of enlightenment), helped bring about the fall of his government (not necessarily bad) and the succession to power by the Ayatollahs (which certainly was bad for Iran and for the United States).

Virtually uncritical U.S. support of Batista, Somoza and countless other tinhorn "Mission Impossible" dictators has caused the unsophisticated working class and peasant populations in those countries to identify the United States, fairly or not, with their very real, everyday personal problems: clear class distinctions and the contrast of a great opulence enjoyed by a few with the tarpaper shacks and hunger of the many; little hope for social or economic advancement, creating a perpetual, transgenerational despair; beatings, torture, imprisonment, and murder for attempting to exercise those political and social rights we ostensibly believe they were born with.

When such regimes fall, as they inevitably do, one of two things happens: If the guerrillas who take control are Marxists, the resulting government will be anti-American and will have the support, on this point, at least, of an anti-Yankee populace. On the other hand, even if those who take control are non-Marxists, they will still be individuals nurtured on distrust or hatred of the United States; the new regime thus will be neutral at best or aligned with the Soviets at worst. In either case, the shortsightedness of our uncritical support of totalitarian *or* authoritarian governments does, and always will, come back to haunt us. We support the South Africas, Chiles, Batista Cubas, Pahlevi Irans, Somoza Nicaraguas at our own risk, buying short-term advantage at a very high long-term cost.

We must maintain our national security. The first priority of the government is to keep its citizens alive and free. That being a given, the foreign policy redirection undertaken by the Reagan administration is both right and necessary. It is essential, however, that the redirection be undertaken with a sophisticated concern for long-range effect. Otherwise we may keep America secure in the 1980s but plant the seeds for even greater dangers in the 1990s and beyond. We must keep America secure not only for ourselves, but for our children as well.

The issue is the extent to which the United States should support regimes that, although "friendly" toward the United States, do not guarantee their citizens the political freedoms characteristic of the Western democracies. Although not a new problem, it is one that was intensified in the closing years of the 1970s with the fall of the Shah of Iran and General Somoza in Nicaragua, and the escalating civil war in El Salvador. Those events bring into sharp focus the problem of reconciling the need for national security with a concern for promoting democracy and human rights in countries to which we lend our support.

Underscoring the importance of the debate is the fact that the United States continues to maintain and is now moving to strengthen ties with countries that, though of considerable importance to American security interests, are far less than democratic. Some contain critical minerals on which we rely to meet the needs of industry and defense. Some are adjacent to sea lanes critically important to commerce and to our national defense. Others are geographically near the United States or its allies, and therefore of potential strategic importance militarily.

But there is another factor to consider. Third World countries that combine a pro-Western political orientation with a determined opposition either to Marxism as a philosophy or communism as a totalitarian reality attain an importance reaching beyond such tangible physical considerations as oil, minerals, and military bases. A country that possesses the will to resist Marxist "liberation" movements represents a valuable asset to the liberal democracies and serves as an inhibition to Communist expansion. What happens in one country has an impact on what happens in others in the region. It is, therefore, imperative to encourage those pro-Western governments that inhibit the spread of Communism.

What emerges is this rule of thumb: A government supportive of the United States and opposed to communism should have a *prima facie* claim *to be considered* for American support and assistance. Three factors justify such a policy:

First, Marxist/Communist movements in the Third World are invariably anti-American.

Second, they typically deny human rights to the citizens of countries under their control.

Third, Marxist regimes tend to be linked by ideology, treaty arrangements, and economic, military, and security assistance to the Soviet Union, East Germany, Cuba, and other Communist nations. The result is a network that constitutes a formidable aggregate threat to U.S. interests.

But while the United States is justified in being predisposed to aid regimes opposed to communism, it would be foolish to adopt a policy of *automatically* granting such regimes our unqualified support. If there is a presumption that such support should be given, it is a rebuttable presumption. One must take other factors into account.

Many Third World countries are strongly authoritarian. Their rulers often use strict measures to maintain their power. We should recognize the danger involved in a policy of supporting non-Communist but undemocratic regimes and consider that it may be imprudent in the long run for the United States to support repressive regimes even though they may be anti-Communist.

Government repression allows Marxists and other radicals to employ the rhetoric of human rights to justify their claim that governments lack legitimacy and should be overthrown while creating widespread popular dissatisfaction with those in power. To be effective, a policy of resisting Communist expansion must acknowledge this danger and face it squarely. Blind support for every anti-communist regime allows passion to substitute for prudence. It risks winning the battle but losing the war.

When formulating U.S. policy toward friendly but flawed regimes, we must determine the direction in which the government desiring our support is moving. If a regime can provide tangible evidence of positive change for the better, then the United States should continue to support it. While we should understand that such efforts can be complicated and temporarily interrupted by the need for dealing with violence and terrorism, it is equally important to stress that we are nonetheless *insistent* on democratic reforms and require that an honest effort toward them is being made.

It is essential that we take care not to undermine the regime's confidence in our resolve to reduce its vulnerability to Communist pressures from without and within; it is as a friend and ally that we can have the greatest effect upon the internal policies of such countries. But if a regime does not show signs of moving toward democracy—if it persists in actions and policies that will destroy its popular support and ultimately lead to its downfall—the United States should be prepared to reduce its support to that government. If it still persists in the trend, we must consider the wisdom of disassociating ourselves from it.

Much of the recent discussion of U.S. support for undemocratic regimes centers on the basic difference between totalitarian and authoritarian regimes.

The distinction is not hard to grasp. A totalitarian government attempts to exercise total, unrestrained control over the lives of its citizens by whatever means necessary. Totalitarianism blurs the distinction between public and private spheres, clearing the way for government intrusion into every dimension of an individual's life. As Hannah Arendt has observed, "It is the very nature of totalitarian regimes to demand unlimited power. Such power can only be secured if literally all men, without a single exception, are reliably dominated in every aspect of their life."

In contrast, authoritarian regimes seek to maintain a monopoly on political activity as traditionally understood. Participation in the political process and in decisions affecting public policy is severely limited. Opposition to the regime, even if nonviolent, brings reprisal. Typically, however, authoritarian regimes allow for a significantly larger degree of freedom in nonpolitical arenas than do totalitarian systems.

Clearly not all undemocratic governments are *uniformly* evil; some are worse than others. When faced with the unpleasant necessity of supporting an authoritarian regime in order to forestall the imposition of a totalitarian one, we need not be paralyzed with indecision. Because the domination is not total in an authoritarian system, the opportunity is present for it to move towards a more democratic arrangement within a framework of stability. This same opportunity is not present within totalitarian regimes. Clearly there is a legitimate basis for sometimes supporting an authoritarian government if the likely alternative would be even worse.

Nevertheless, too much can be made of the distinction. Having decided to support an authoritarian regime as a check against the totalitarian alternative, the United States must take care not to give the impression that it is comfortable with regimes that show no inclination towards democracy. Being pro-West is not equivalent to being pro-democracy. The United States must signal in an unambiguous way that it strongly desires authoritarian regimes to enlarge the scope of civil and political liberties, and it must emphasize that when it supports authoritarian regimes it does so out of prudence and not out of principle. Moreover, when an authoritarian regime by its actions warrants the hostility of the majority of its citizens, prudence may well dictate that the United States distance itself from the regime.

American foreign policy towards its Third World allies must strike a delicate balance between sensitivity to their security needs (and ours) and our insistence that there be measurable progress toward expanding political liberty. Obviously, this is a policy easier to state than to implement, and considerable care will be required to avoid the pitfalls of the past.

For example, U.S. insistence on internal reform, even if not destabilizing to a regime, is sometimes counterproductive. As a result of public condemnation by the Carter administration of Brazil's human rights record, that country terminated a U.S. naval mission of long standing and declined to participate in a cooperative effort to frustrate Soviet encroachment on the South Atlantic sea lanes.

In addition, U.S. policymakers cannot afford to be complacent about the very real danger that withdrawal of American support for a regime aligned with the United States might facilitate the rise to power of a government that is both hostile to America and even more oppressive than the one it replaces. Judging from the way events have unfolded it seems evident that this is what has happened in post-revolutionary Iran and Nicaragua.

Since Khomeini ascended to power in Iran, more than 1,000 executions have been reported. Trials have typically been charades with the accused denied access to counsel or the time to prepare a defense. It is legitimate to wonder whether the Iranian people are better off now than they were under the Shah.

The record of the Sandinista government in Nicaragua prompts serious doubts about whether the Sandinistas constitute an improvement over Somoza's rule. According to the president of the Nicaraguan Permanent Commission on Human Rights, at least 500 illegal executions and perhaps as many as 1,000 were carried out by the Sandinista guerillas in their first six months of power. Estimates of the number of political prisoners have ranged from 5,000 to as many as 12,000. National elections have been postponed until 1985 in a country no longer plagued by civil war.

Trends in Iran and Nicaragua should alert us to what is likely to happen when the U.S. withdraws support from its authoritarian allies.

The decisive political conflict in our century is that between totalitarian communism and liberal democracy. To meet the challenge adequately, United States foreign policy must be two-pronged. First, it must be impacably opposed to the expansion of communism. Second, U.S. policy must protect and nurture democratic governments where they now exist and encourage their emergence where they do not. It would be an error in political judgment to concentrate *all* of our attention on what the Communists are doing, while totally ignoring the social and political shortcomings of pro-Western, undemocratic regimes.

Dictatorships unsupported by the people inevitably fall, and if we permit the United States to be seen as the principal prop for those regimes we will be confronted when they fall with government and public sentiment against the United States. Emphasis on containment of the immediate communist threat is a valid basis for a short-term foreign policy, but long-term policy requires a concerted effort to see to it that we do not sow the seeds for even worse trouble in the future.

5. Firemen and Visionaries

The Nature of the Congress tends to focus the attention of its members on the crisis of the moment. Immediate problems take precedence over simmering problems. Unlike the books on the *New York Times* weekly bestseller list, which inch their way slowly upward in the public attention, gradually displacing previous bestsellers as they run their course, some political issues spring to life and quickly take positions of prominence. Issues which are low in priority tend to remain there, never receiving full attention until they have developed into crises which threaten to boil over.

The result is a failure by the Congress to come to grips with issues which may prove in the long run to be of immense importance in shaping the future quality of our lives.

Theodore Lowi, in his book, *The End of Liberalism*, writes of what he calls "possibly self-destructive aspects of capitalism."

"Capitalism," Lowi says, "produces industrialization and urbanization. These two phenomena are the sources of stress and strains that will not necessarily be solved by more capitalism, industrialization and urbanization. Yet to have less of them would require interference with the natural tendency of a market-governed economy to expand."

As industrialization depersonalizes and urbanization destroys privacy, as the quality of life erodes, we who believe in a freedom-oriented economy need to turn our attention to keeping capitalism's incentives alive without making life so miserable that everybody gets to have a bigger and bigger share of a less and less enjoyable life.

Tom Robbins, in a very different kind of book, *Still Life With Woodpecker*, writes: "The problem starts at the secondary level, not with the originator or developer of the idea but with the people who are attracted by it, who adopt it, who cling to it until their last nail breaks, and who invariably lack the overview, flexibility, imagination, and, most importantly, sense of humor, to maintain it in the spirit in which it was hatched."

Adam Smith's was the mind that devised in the 1700s a system of economics that offered unparalleled and unprecedented hope for progress by unleashing the desire for personal profit in a way that would produce, along with that personal profit, great gain for the society as a whole and the people in it. It has worked its miracles. But it is a *living* idea and as it grows, new problems emerge and must be dealt with. We are inheritors not of dogma but of ideas, and we must from time to time focus on those ideas and adapt them to new problems, new perceptions of our needs, keeping those ideas serving us, rather than the other way around. Yet when do we find time to elevate those concerns to a first priority?

Progress turns backward villages without electric power, without telephones, without medical facilities, into modern cities with conveniences and luxuries, and then more "progress" turns those cities into jungles full of traffic jams, long lines at theaters and restaurants and grocery store checkout counters, and streets and sidewalks on which one is likely to be mugged and robbed. Each step brings new problems to be dealt with.

The population grows older as science prolongs life. New technologies make old manufacturing facilities obsolete, and the population shifts from the manufacturing centers of the north and east to the sunbelt cities of the south and west. Each change brings new problems that demand new solutions—shifting water from areas that have it to areas that do not; maintaining old cities on a shrinking tax base and building new cities to handle problems that never existed before.

How well America can meet those challenges, how well we can shape the agenda for the eighties, will determine not our survival but the quality of life—whether or not survival will be pleasant.

Can we set aside the *politics* of education—the demand for more money, higher salaries, new gymnasiums—to focus our attention on the need to improve the *quality* of education?

Can we revise the laws governing federal agencies to turn them again into servants of the public will rather than impersonal order-givers?

Can we devise a foreign policy and build alliances that will stand the test of time rather than merely dealing with the exigencies of the moment through a series of expedient but short-sighted stop-gap containments?

Can we find ways to structure the private sector so it can meet the needs of the society? Or will heat be turned off in the winter and lonely widows be left to freeze to death because government charity is too expensive and private charity has forgotten them?

Can we find ways to open the private enterprise system to blacks and women in a way that will provide them with meaningful opportunity?

The list of "can we" thises and thats, unfortunately, is longer than the list of issues upon which we in the Congress focus our attention, longer than the list of priorities on the public agenda.

Every nation needs its firemen, dousing the flames of the latest crisis. But it also needs its dreamers, its visionaries, its planners, its hopers, its builders. For the past 50 years we conservatives have been the firemen; liberals have done the hoping, planning, dreaming. Their dreams have been wonderful; their plans have been imperfect; the need for firemen has been great. But at least they dreamed. Fifty years of liberal schemes have proven that bigger and bigger government is not the way to create the Utopia that inspired the schemes that made government bigger and bigger. Liberalism has tried and it has failed. But if we conservatives are to inherit the mantle of leadership and keep it for a while, we, too, must dream.

On April 2, 1980, soon after William Casey succeeded John Sears as Ronald Reagan's campaign manager. I wrote Casey, suggesting some thoughts to be included in the candidate's campaign speeches:

"I think John Connally is right when he perceives that the people want a 'leader,' but I believe he is mistaken about what kind of leadership they want. I really don't think the American people are looking for a 'strong man' so much as they are looking for somebody with a vision and the ability to inspire. They are looking, still, for what Jack Kennedy and Bobby Kennedy offered in their rhetoric—a vision of a better America. For many Americans that boils down to this: removing the artificial obstacles which stand in the way of their achieving their own individual dreams."

There are critical problems to be faced up to in the 1980s. We must begin to deal with the shaping of a society that we will want our children to live in.

Part Four
SOMETHING TO BELIEVE IN

Part Four
SOMETHING TO BELIEVE IN

CHAPTER NINE
CROSSROADS QUESTIONS

To Inez Milholland

Upon this marble bust that is not I
Lay the round, formal wreath that is not fame;
But in the forum of my silenced cry
Root ye the living tree whose sap is flame.
I, that was proud and valiant, am no more;—
Save as a dream that wanders wide and late,
Save as a wind that rattles the stout door,
Troubling the ashes in the sheltered grate.
The stone will perish; I shall be twice dust.
Only my standard on a taken hill
Can cheat the mildew and the red-brown rust
And make immortal my adventurous will.
Even now the silk is tugging at the staff.
Take up the song; forget the epitaph.

—Edna St. Vincent Millay

1. A Matter of Principle

On August 18, 1982, I sat in the East Room of the White House with tears in my eyes. In front of me a President I had worked for, a man I care for, was openly pleading for my help.

There were 40 of us in the room that day—40 conservatives in rebellion against the President's campaign to raise taxes by more than $220 billion over the next five years, the largest tax increase in the nation's history.

We were surrounded by the President's top advisors—our friends—and by our own party leadership. Less than a week before, I had been part of a much smaller group sitting around the table in the Cabinet room with the President. That day I sat two seats away from Ronald Reagan and the plea was just as intense then and much more personal.

The first meeting—the smaller meeting—had been with what the President called his Core Group in the House of Representatives, a dozen or so House members, led by Delaware Congressman Tom Evans, who had been the President's earliest and closest supporters. We had campaigned for Ronald Reagan from one end of the country to the other. I had personally campaigned for him in the snow and ice of New Hampshire, in the southern part of Florida, from Fort Lauderdale to Miami to the Keys, on college campuses from Southern Illinois to Lehigh, and I had been one of two Congressmen in the motel room with Reagan and his wife, Nancy, when they received confirmation that they had won the New Hampshire primary after an earlier loss to George Bush in Iowa.

There were memories—many of them—of close ties with the President. Four of us in the Core Group—Evans, Jack Kemp, Carroll Campbell and myself—had served as well on a small committee called the Thursday Night Group, which met under the leadership of Evans, Senator Paul Laxalt, and Richard Allen (later the President's national security advisor) to assist the campaign strategists with input from a Washington perspective. I had served as a director of a campaign advisory team which included 20 different issues task forces, each chaired by a Senator and a House Member. My ties with Ronald Reagan were real and they were personal. And they were long-standing. He and I had known each other for many years and I had called him at home in California on the night of his loss in Iowa to let him know that I was ready to join his campaign team in an active way. Since he had been President I had been a loyal member of the Reagan team, almost always in the forefront of speaking for and campaigning for the President's initiatives. I had opposed him—and opposed him vigorously—on his endorsement of a $12 billion foreign aid bill, but that was a rare difference of opinion.

And then some differences—some very real differences—had begun to appear. Conservatives—the President's friends and supporters—began to find gaps they could not bridge between White House policy and their own—our own—political consciences.

The first of those breaks had come over the White House-approved Republican alternative budget proposal in early 1982. In trying to hold moderate and liberal Republicans in a coalition that would give the President enough votes to win on the House floor, the White House had agreed to a budget plan that included a deficit of approximately $110 billion. My first reaction was one of shock, and I had told my supporters and the press that I could not go along with such an enormous, built-in, projected, expected, approved deficit.

I soon found that many others on the House floor agreed with me. At least four Republican Members of the House Ways and Means Committee (the Committee that would have to devise the tax plans to produce new revenues)—John Rousselot, of California, Bill Archer, of Texas, Jim Martin, of North Carolina, and Phil Crane, of Illinois—were strongly opposed to the budget.

Under Archer's leadership we began to gather in small meeting rooms—first in his office and then, as we grew, in a variety of Committee hearing rooms—and began to dissect the budget. The deficit had to be trimmed sharply, we agreed—below $100 billion in any case—and spending cutbacks, if they were to have public support, would have to be equitable.

With those guidelines we began to look at the entire federal budget, line by line and item by item. Other Members began to join us—Martin; Crane; Crane's younger brother, Dan, (also a Congressman from Illinois); Dan Lungren, John Rousselot, Bobbi Fiedler and Bill Dannemeyer from California; Denny Smith from Oregon; Ed Bethune from Arkansas; Newt Gingrich from Georgia; Bob Walker and Dick Schulze from Pennsylvania—soon more than seventy Conservatives, including almost all of Reagan's earliest supporters.

By the time the budget came to the floor we were meeting almost around the clock, every day, and had come to a general agreement that we could not permit the Republican budget then on the floor to be passed. Our complaints to the Republican leadership had gone unheeded. There was a general belief among the leadership and at the

White House that we conservatives would have nowhere else to go and would have to support the Republican plan.

We decided it was important to send a signal that would let Bob Michel, the Republican leader in the House, and the President know how many of us there were and how seriously we were committed to improving the budget. Dan Crane suggested that on the next amendment vote, whatever it was, we all merely vote "present" rather than "yes" or "no," and allow those strange and rare yellow lights to remain on the board throughout most of the 15 minutes of the vote before we each switched to cast the votes that accurately reflected our individual positions.

The strategy worked. When the bells rang, we rushed up the one flight of stairs to the House floor and punched in our perforated plastic voting cards. One after another we voted "present". Twenty, thirty, forty, fifty, sixty of us. Except on a quorum call I had never before seen more than a handful of "present" votes on any issue before the House. Members began coming up to us to ask what the protest was about. They began to join us and the numbers began to swell.

Later we switched our votes. The strategy worked. We drew public attention to the presence of a large dissident element within Republican ranks.

The next day, David Broder of the *Washington Post,* reflecting on the proliferation of yellow lights, dubbed us "The Yellowjackets," to be added to the growing House menagerie which then already included the "Boll Weevils"—conservative southern Democrats—and the "Gypsy Moths"—liberal northeastern Republicans. To Michel, however, we pointed out that unlike either of those groups, both of which functioned by trying to tug their own parties away from the consensus viewpoint of the party's membership—we represented the bulk of Republican thought in the House and were merely trying to keep the party from straying away from its majority opinion in order to form coalitions with liberal splinter elements. Michel agreed and, despite Broder's more colorful phrase, the House leadership began to refer to us as "The Regulars."

Whatever we were called—and at the White House, where the deals had been made, the terms may have been far less flattering then either "Regulars" or "Yellowjackets"—our point had been made.

Most of us voted against the Republican budget plan, as well as the Democratic plan, which was even worse, and both plans went down to defeat. Within hours, half a dozen of us were seated in Michel's office in the Capitol, included for the first time in the strategy sessions designed to produce a new Republican budget plan. In the days that followed, we met continuously with Michel, Republican whip Trent Lott, and at the White House with the President and his top budget strategists—Treasury Secretary Donald Regan, Budget Director David Stockman, and key assistants to the President, including Jim Baker and Ed Meese.

Our insistence on a reduced deficit and larger spending cuts produced some improvement—a saving of nearly $10 billion—and the next Republican budget alternative was passed by the House, but some of us still could not support it.

Although we had decided to keep the Yellowjackets together for the fights that would invariably follow, the press of Congressional business, committee work and the rapidly-approaching elections kept us from any consistent effort to mold the group into a permanent organization.

And then the President, first in a statement at the White House and then in a speech from the West Steps of the Capitol, endorsed a tax package put together by Senator Robert Dole and the members of the Senate Finance Committee.

That tax package mobilized a conservative rebellion. The President's endorsement was based on a belief that the size of the projected deficit would prevent interest rates from coming down and that only a sizable tax increase designed to trim that deficit could bring about real economic recovery. It was a view he held, and holds, with great conviction.

We, on the other hand, believed that the early signs of recovery—increased retail sales, increased personal savings, sharp reductions in inflation, a 25 percent drop in interest rates—were a reflection, at least in part, of the reductions in federal tax rates the year before, and that a sizable tax increase would slow the recovery.

In the two meetings with the President I had argued for a major campaign led by the President to force the Congress to cut back on "entitlement"spending—automatic increases in social programs which already totaled more than $175 billion a year, exclusive of social security costs. They were good programs which had grown beyond all proportion—guaranteed student loans available now to the children of parents making more than $100,000 a year; black lung disease benefits for people who were not required to prove they had black lung disease; food stamps for college students whose parents were affluent.

While the White House had sharply criticized the programs—and the very nature of entitlements, which permits annual cost-of-living increases that bypass the Congressional appropriation process—no serious effort to mount a campaign had been made either in the Congress or among the public to bring such programs into line.

We had been elected, I argued, on a platform promising to cut taxes and to cut spending. Instead we had made no real dent in entitlement spending and the spending reductions we had made, because they had come out of the 40 percent of the budget which Congress deals with each year (entitlements—the other 60 percent—cannot be changed without basic revisions in the law) were inequitable and tended to emasculate some programs and seriously damage others, including many of the programs for the elderly and the handicapped which could most reasonably be justified even in a time of shrinking federal beneficence.

The President, however, had made a public commitment. As White House aides—and eventually even the President—put it, there was more at stake now than whether the House passed a tax increase or not; the President's credibility and leadership ability were at stake.

I love Ronald Reagan as a man—he is open, sincere and honest—and I share his basic political philosophy—more reliance on the private sector and less on government—but it was an argument I had heard before.

At one meeting at the White House, Lyn Nofziger, the President's retired political advisor (who had returned temporarily to run the campaign for the tax increase, after first opposing it) told of a conversation he had just had with former President Richard Nixon.

Nixon had told him, Nofziger said, that if the United States had had a parliamentary system, and if the Prime Minister had submitted a major tax bill and his own party had voted against him, that would be the same as a vote of no confidence.

Presumably Nofziger's story was meant to impress upon us the necessity of showing our confidence in the President's leadership. But of course this was not Britain, and many of us felt—and feel—that we in the Congress properly owe our allegiance to those who elect us and not to any President, regardless of his charisma, character or political platform.

The days that followed were hard and bitter ones—among the hardest I have known as a member of Congress. Tempers flared and in meetings at the White House, Nofziger and the President's chief Congressional liaison, Ken Duberstein, became short-tempered and sharp-tongued. An assistant at the Republican National Committee, Richard Bond, according to the *Wall Street Journal*, warned that if members of Congress did not go along with the President he (Bond) would see to it that they were cut off at the knees. The President, in a speech in Utah, referred to "jackasses" in Washington. One wire service story suggested that he was talking about people—mostly Republicans—who opposed the tax increase legislation. The next day, House conservatives entered the chambers wearing large green and white buttons proclaiming "Another JACKASS Against Tax Hikes."

I had originally decided to keep out of the fight, although I was planning to vote against the bill. In meetings of the Republican whip organization, I had explained that even though I was an assistant whip I could not support the bill and could not help line up votes for it (which is the whip's primary responsibility), but I remained low-key and quiet about my opposition

As the battle went on, however, I found myself drawn more and more into the center of the fight. I am national chairman of the American Conservative Union and in deference to that organization's more than 300,000 members and active supporters, who were outspoken in opposition to the tax increase, ACU could not remain silent. The board of directors agreed to campaign against the bill.

As more of the leadership role fell to me, I began to conduct daily strategy sessions in my office, meeting with Ed Bethune, Newt Gingrich, Dan Lungren, Bob Walker and John Rousselot, and staying in touch by phone with Jack Kemp, who was a principal spokesman against tax increases but wanted to avoid turning this battle into a Kemp-Reagan controversy.

As the vote neared, we realized that we did not have a whip organization of our own, so I began to set one up, assigning key opponents of the bill to work with other members whose votes might be won and keeping a running tally of where the vote stood at all times, updating the counts on a twice-a-day basis.

Three times in a week I met with representatives from a score of conservative organizations, reviewing what each was doing to generate mail and telephone calls from members across the country in opposition to the tax increase, and suggesting new strategies.

It was in the midst of this struggle that I sat in the East Room, unable to look away from the President as he pleaded for support. It was an emotional moment and not for the first time that week I had tears in my eyes as I realized the personal stake the President had in this battle. I felt he was wrong, I could not support him, but I agonized just the same.

Eventually the President won, although if we had switched the votes of only 11 members *we* would have won. It was a close battle and one that could have easily torn the Republican Party apart.

Instead it was a victory for the party, a day of a new maturity. In the heat of battle—an emotional and traumatic battle for almost every Republican in the House—we had proved we could go through a divisive struggle without being divided. Jack Kemp, as chairman of the House Republican Conference—and a passionate opponent of tax increases—had been scrupulously fair in allowing the Conference to be used as a sounding board for both sides of the debate. Trent Lott, the Republican whip, had used his own considerable persuasiveness on Republican members to win support for the President's position, but had refused to force the whip organization, which was badly divided, to play a role. Bob Michel, the Republican leader, had listened fairly to both sides and refrained form applying pressure. Barber Conable, the Republican floor manager for the tax increase, had divided his time equally between advocates of the increase and its opponents, permitting those of us who opposed the bill to choose our own speakers and allocate the time among them.

It was a time of great growth for the Republican Party. But it was also a time of great decision for Republican conservatives. Before the tax fight we had been, except on rare occasions, the President's troops to command. No longer was that so. Politics is based on principle, not personality. Republican conservatives admire and respect Ronald Reagan and had taken far longer to declare their independence of him than had been the case with a Nixon or a Ford in the White House. But independence is an essential of political integrity. In the future, Ronald Reagan will have the support of most conservatives most of the time, just as he has had in the past, but the support will probably be less automatic and the challenges less traumatic.

2. Computers and Demographics: The Triumph of Pragmatism

Back in 1944, a Chinese philosopher and writer, Dr. Lin Yutang, attempting to explain the vast gulf between Chinese and Western phi-

losophies, described what he called "the difference between the approach of facts and the approach of values."

Western philosophers, he suggested, seem to think the human mind is like an adding machine; if you put all the facts into the machine, you automatically draw out the correct answer.

Chinese humanism, on the other hand, he said, concentrates "on human values...the values of human relationships."

It was a perceptive analysis of the atrophy of Western thought, and what he observed in Western philosophy in general is even more valid in political philosophy in particular. Philosophical considerations have all but disappeared from American politics, which is one of the reasons that the few men in public life who are perceived to have a burning vision—the Martin Luther Kings, for example, the Ronald Reagans, the Barry Goldwaters, and the Hubert Humphreys—stand out so clearly from the pack. Philosophy, goals, visions have been too often replaced by a vague sort of pragmatism that is only peripherally connected with any of the broader concepts of what politics used to be all about.

"Political philosophy" has, in fact, become the art of operating a non-ideological adding machine (or computer), measuring rates, trends, attitudes and assorted demographic statistics.

Of the eight post-war Presidents, only three, Truman, Kennedy, and Reagan can arguably be said to represent some sort of ingrained political idealism, and it may be stretching a point to say it of either Kennedy or Truman.

But of the other five, there can be no doubt: political ideology— and that can be carried to include a belief in creation of a certain idealistic sort of society—had very little to do with the presidency or the persuit of it.

Despite the differences in party affiliation (which is an almost meaningless consideration) and "gut-level,"instinctive, reactions to specific issues, Eisenhower, Johnson, Nixon, Ford and Carter represented the ultimate triumph of pragmatic politics.

Ironically, all but Eisenhower had some sort of label attached to them to indicate what specific sub-branch of which philosophy they represented. The chances are none of them understood or cared what the theorists were talking about.

Richard Nixon and Spiro Agnew, for example, were considered by the press and the intellectual community to be "conservatives," labels political conservatives disavowed many years before Watergate or the surfacing of Agnew's Maryland past.

Perhaps the single most important philosophical (or non-philosophical) truth about the fall of Nixon and Agnew is the one called "cause and effect." It means, politically, that the cracks and chinks and flaws which led Mr. Nixon to his seventh and last crisis, and Mr. Agnew to his only one, were there all along; that Watergate and income tax evasion should come as a surprise only to those who hadn't been looking.

Those whose job it was to analyze and comment upon such matters as Watergate and the Agnew affair missed the one truly significant aspect of both, and that is one they share at their very roots. What has happened is simply that pragmatism has been found out. In both cases, pragmatic men did the pragmatic thing.

Nothing happened to America (despite the incessant breast-beating of those who excel in that sort of thing); it was simply the truth coming home to roost. It was not that America was in trouble; the American political system as it has evolved in the past quarter-century was in trouble.

America is not at fault for the fact that Richard Nixon, who may have been the most non-ideological president of a pragmatic age, assembled about himself a breed of men incapable of distinguishing between "tough" politics and criminal activity. Nor is America to blame because Spiro Agnew was violating the law even as he won the public's applause by denouncing lawlessness. Those are the faults of Mr. Nixon and Mr. Agnew, and faults for which no other single individual can be made to share the blame.

What should be blamed, however, besides those two men themselves, is the disastrous trend in American politics to place "winning" above principle in political priority; to make it "safe" to believe in nothing, and controversial to believe in something; to elevate pragmatism to a qualification for office.

It is not enough that a candidate has as his chief virtue that he will not alienate and therefore "can win"; Watergate and the Agnew affair demonstrated, if nothing else, that it was time somebody started believing in something, started putting principle above expediency, philosophy above pragmatism.

Mr. Nixon, it must be remembered, never sat well with the party that three times nominated him. For one thing, for too long he defied political description. To liberals, he was a rightist; to conservatives, he was often suspect of being a liberal with conservative rhetoric. Somehow Mr. Nixon managed always to find supporters on both left and right—Senators Goldwater, Thurmond and Tower among conservatives, for example—and those supporters would then explain to their followers that they had talked with Nixon and had come away convinced that deep within he was one of them; that, in his heart, they knew he was right; that at a convenient time in the future he would come forth as the champion of their common cause.

When he attained the presidency, conservatives waited in vain for the "real" Richard Nixon to emerge. (Waited in vain, that is, until Watergate.) Instead, he proposed national health insurance, guaranteed annual incomes and wage and price controls. Liberals could take no heart, however, for he was at the same time nominating a succession of Carswells and Hayneworths to sit on the Supreme Court.

When the real Richard Nixon refused to stand up, neutral observers concluded that he was a centrist. It is with Mr. Nixon as it is with trick mirrors; it all depends on the viewing angle. But Mr. Nixon was not a centrist, either, for that indicates the existence of a political philosophy somewhere between conservatism and liberalism, between libertarianism and statism. In truth, Mr. Nixon had no philosophy at all, not even a centrist one. His actions were based on the political polls. Even as he said: "It would, of course, be the easier course (to do otherwise)" he would, in fact, be pursuing "the easier course," defying public wrath to do that which polls had already told him the public would support.

What Watergate and Mr. Agnew revealed is the extent to which even the professed principles of the Nixon administration—the overriding concern for lawfulness, for example—were simply set aside to ensure for the President and Vice President their most important philosophical goal: re-election.

Presidents Johnson and Kennedy might have been equally as willing to employ similar tactics; after all, there was ample evidence all along that the White House during those administrations made effective use of its resident power to ensure the incumbent's hold on his office.

But this is not a defense of Richard Nixon; it's an indictment of the political trend. Nixon, Ford, Johnson and Carter could best be described as essentially pragmatic centrists (i.e., men with no discernable philosophy, other than an occasional bias one way or another)—and probably even the term "centrist" ascribes too much position to them.

It is the Agnews and the Nixons who have been the true symbols of current American political thought, just as the Johnsons were before them. Senator Goldwater and Senator McGovern were perceived by the electorate as too extreme, in opposite directions, and both were rejected by overwhelming margins. The result in both cases was a predictable one: a swing toward the "middle" (i.e., toward non-philosophy) by both parties.

After the 1964 defeat of Senator Goldwater, Republicans throughout the country began to talk of the need for a candidate "who could win"; principle was all but abandoned, except in unread party platforms and the hope that Richard Nixon would prove, after all, to be a conservative. There was no cry of "wait 'till next year"; instead there was a quick scurrying for cover by embarrassed promoters of the Goldwater candidacy, and a re-emergence of the vindicated pragmatists who could still not control the delegate-selection process, but who could now cow conservatives into going along with a "winner" in exchange for a mere whisper of hope that he would turn out okay. Ronald Reagan was the new conservative hero, but Richard Nixon was all but uncontested for the 1968 nomination and not primarily because of Reagan's indecision in starting the race. The same thing happened in the Democratic Party (by then Humphrey had ceased to be the party's ideological hero: he did, however, become the party's nominee).

The Watergate break-in and the Agnew resignation had a significance beyond themselves and beyond the reforms they brought about in the political process. They were proof that cause and effect relationships exist as surely in politics as elsewhere, for both incidents were the natural results of pursuing non-political politics; of putting in our highest offices men who cannot spell out a clear-cut philosophy of government, but whose actions are guided, instead, only by the exigencies—and the opportunities—of the moment.

America is at a crossroads; in fact, America is *always* at a crossroads. What do we do now?

From time to time, I receive letters from angry constituents demanding to know why we in the Congress don't quit "playing games"—our prolonged disputes, for example, over the makeup of the federal budget—and get down to business. But, of course, these are not games and we are not playing. The month-long standoff in the debate over the 1983 fiscal budget was more than a case of Ronald Reagan and Tip O'Neill debating whether to play "Annie Over" or "Kick the

Can;" it was a major and historic confrontation over the direction in which the country was to move, and only in a society conditioned by television to expect instant answers could such a significant debate be characterized as a meaningless waste of time. From Ronald Reagan's viewpoint, the Tip O'Neills of the world are responsible for destroying much of the American dream he had learned about in smalltown Illinois. From the Speaker's standpoint, Ronald Reagan was systematically destroying everything Tip O'Neill believed in.

At stake were fundamental issues: Should the federal government expand its control over social and welfare programs or should more power be turned back to state and local governments; should individuals and businesses pay more in taxes to pay for more government or should the tax burden be reduced so individuals could achieve their aspirations and businesses could expand to produce more and create more jobs for more people; should the national defense be treated as another line-item in the budget, competing with food stamps and housing subsidies for priority, or was providing for the national defense a *sine qua non* of government, a first priority, a *raison d'etre?*

These decisions are more than "important;" they are "crossroads" questions. These debates do not call for adding machines, computer printouts and econometric models; they call for passion, for commitment, for principles, for vision.

The triumph of pragmatism in 20th century American politics has created a government obsessed with instant, simple solutions... regulating the design of toilet seats, for example. The 21st century will require something better.

3. A Last Word

One Sunday last September I was thinking about a call I had just received from a constituent in Oklahoma City. A bank had failed and through a series of events he was about to lose sixty million dollars and would be bankrupt.

As I thought about it, about whether there was anything I could do to help, I scrubbed harder and harder. My constituent wanted to know if I could properly do anything to save his 60 million; Lisa and I had just moved to a new rental house and I was scrubbing the inside of the oven at the old house to save the $100 cleaning fee we would have had to pay if we had left the work for the landlord.

Later the same month I was on the telephone with a constituent in a new part of my Congressional district (the redistricting by the state legislature had added six new counties to the district). He was saying that it was time I did something for the people in his town. He was aware of the work I had done to oppose an increase in his taxes, to re-build the national defense system that protected his family and com-munity, but because he had *agreed* with my votes, that (his support for what I was doing) was something *he* had done for *me* and not some-thing I had done for him; therefore I owed him one.

There's nothing quite like life in the Congress. It's amusing, annoying, confusing and infinitely more satisfying than almost any other human endeavor, except for the ministry. This is where one ac-tually gets to try to be the man he once hoped he would be. It's a plat-form from which one can see the weaknesses in the fiber of the country and fashion the repairs to strengthen it. It's a stage from which to shape programs to help the poor, to see obstacles to opportu-nity and remove them, to strengthen our ability to withstand aggres-sion by those who would destroy this uniquely free society.

Behind enemy lines? Maybe. But it's also the front lines. What America is now is what previous Congresses and millions of Ameri-cans have made it. What it will be for our children is what you and I will make it. Let us dream our dreams of the future; we can make them come true.